What to feed when

annabel karmel

What to feed when

More than 300 Q&As & 50 delicious recipes

LONDON, NEW YORK, MUNICH,
MELBOURNE, DELHI

Project editor Helen Murray
Recipe editor Norma MacMillan
Designer Jo Grey
Senior art editor Sarah Ponder
Design assistant and jacket designer
  Charlotte Seymour
Managing editors Esther Ripley and
  Penny Warren
Managing art editors Marianne Markham and
  Glenda Fisher
Senior production editor Jennifer Murray
Senior production controller Wendy Penn
Creative technical support Sonia Charbonnier
Category publisher Peggy Vance
Recipe testing Caroline Stearns
Editorial consultant Karen Sullivan
Allergy consultant Dr Adam Fox
Breastfeeding consultant Joanna Moorhead
Nutritional consultant Dr Rosan Meyer
Paediatric consultant Dr Su Laurent
Food styling Seiko Hatfield and Katie Giovanni
Home economist Carolyn Humphries
Photographers Dave King and Michael Birt
Photography art direction Carole Ash

First published as *Your Feeding Questions Answered* in
Great Britain in 2009 by Dorling Kindersley Limited
80 Strand, London WC2R 0RL. Penguin Group (UK)

A CIP catalogue record is available from the British Library.

ISBN: 978-1-4053-6208-5

Printed and bound by LEO Paper Group in China

Discover more at
www.dk.com

contents

foreword

As parents, we all worry about whether we're bringing up our children the right way. It's really hard to know what is best: Is it OK to give an occasional bottle if you're breastfeeding your baby? At what age should you introduce solid food? When is the right time to give your baby a cup? How do you know when your little one is ready for finger foods?

I have written this book to guide you through each stage of feeding your baby and toddler, up to three years of age, by answering all the common questions that concern mums. Whatever the problems you may encounter along the way, they are sure to be shared with other mums. Reading this book will give you an insight into what to expect, as well as lots of tips and advice on how to cope with all manner of feeding issues.

Right from the start breastfeeding can be a challenge and it can be easy to give up – especially in those often difficult first few days. However, with the right advice, you will soon find that breastfeeding is much easier and more enjoyable than you ever imagined, so persevere!

Introducing a baby to solid food is a confusing time, as there is so much conflicting advice. I find that parents are often so worried about food allergies that they keep their babies on very restricted diets of fruit and vegetables, because they're concerned about introducing foods such as eggs, fish, and meat. However, babies will not thrive on low-calorie, restricted diets – they need iron from red meat, essential fatty acids from oily fish and, unlike adults, they need more fat and less fibre in their diets. The advice I give in this book is based on the latest medical research from the UK's top experts. I want to give mums and dads the confidence to know that they are giving their babies the food they need to grow and develop.

Since I lost my first child Natasha twenty years ago, I have devoted my life to researching child nutrition. I have written 22 books and I work with the top experts in the field of child nutrition. With the knowledge I have gained over the years, I find ways to encourage children to eat the foods that are good for them by including them in tasty recipes, which are easy to prepare. Combining my own experiences as a mum of three with the latest scientific research, I hope that this book will help to guide you through your baby's first few years, and give you the peace of mind to know that you are giving your child the very best start in life.

Annabel Karmel

chapter 1

0–6 months:
your new baby and you

0–6 months:
what you can expect

Your new baby will gradually settle into a routine of feeding and sleeping, growing more alert and **investigating her world** as she stays awake for longer periods. Your baby will grow more in this period than **at any other time in her life.** Settle in and enjoy the process of bonding.

Q Why is it so important to breastfeed for the first few days?

A While the longer you breastfeed your baby, the greater the benefits, you'll be giving your baby a better start even if you can manage it just for a few days. Breast milk is designed to provide complete nourishment for a baby for at least six months after birth. Before milk is produced a mother's breasts produces colostrum, a deep-yellow liquid containing high levels of protein, nutrients, and antibodies. A newborn baby who feeds on colostrum in the first few days of life is better able to resist the bacteria and viruses that cause illness. Your milk, which begins to flow a few days after childbirth when your hormones change, is a blue-white colour with a thin consistency and provides the perfect balance of nutrients for your baby. Some mums are alarmed that it looks "weak" or even "skimmed" next to the rich, yellowy colour of formula milk, but it is important to remember that it's been designed this way for a reason, and provides easily digestible nutrients that are just right for a baby.

Q How often do babies need to be fed?

A Your baby's appetite and needs will change constantly as she grows and develops, and it is important that she is fed when she is hungry. At the outset, you may be feeding your newborn every two hours or so, but it is almost impossible to overfeed a breastfed baby. For the first month of life, your baby needs between 8 and 12 feeds every day. As she grows and begins to take more at feeding time, she will go a little longer – sometimes up to three or four hours – between feeds. As you get to know your new baby, you'll recognize her signs of hunger, and know when she needs to be fed.

Q Is milk all my baby needs for the first six months?

A Breast milk and/or formula milk are perfectly designed to be a complete food for babies, providing them with nutrients, such as protein, fat, carbohydrates, vitamins and minerals, calories, as well as liquid to keep them hydrated. In the case of breast milk, your baby will get some additional benefits, such as antibodies against infections, as well as hormones, EFAs (essential fatty acids), enzymes, and living cells which fight infection. If you are bottle-feeding, EFAs and other elements, such as probiotics, may also be added to your baby's formula to ensure your baby's health. At present, the UK government and the WHO (World Health Organization) recommend exclusive breastfeeding for six months, but you may feel that your baby is ready for solids a little earlier than this (see pages 40-41). If this is the case, speak to your health visitor or GP.

★ your baby's tummy

Your baby's tummy is smaller than you may think. At birth, it's roughly the size of a chickpea, growing to the size of a cherry in the first week. By four weeks, her tummy will be the size of a walnut, and it remains much the same until she is six months old, when, in most cases, her tummy will be the size of her fist.

the art of breastfeeding

Breastfeeding offers a magical opportunity to develop a close, **intimate bond with your new baby**, and gives him the best possible start to life. Your breast milk provides all of the ingredients he needs for **optimum health, growth, and development**, and has plenty of benefits for you, too.

Q What are the advantages of breastfeeding?

A Breast milk provides a perfect start for your baby, affecting health and development on many different levels. For one thing, the composition of breast milk changes constantly, to allow for your baby's individual growth and changing nutritional needs. Research has found that breastfed babies have fewer incidences of vomiting, diarrhoea, gastroenteritis, as well as other infections and illnesses (it is especially important for premature babies to be breastfed as it strengthens their immune system). Breast milk also reduces the risk of chronic constipation, colic and other tummy disorders, and promotes growth. There is a reduced risk of childhood diabetes in breastfed babies, and they are considerably less likely to become obese or develop heart disease in later life. Research suggests breastfeeding exclusively for six months may protect against allergies, asthma, and eczema. There is also a reduced risk of SIDS (sudden infant death syndrome): research has found that of every 87 deaths from SIDS, only 3 took place in breastfed babies. The emotional benefits are well-documented – breastfed babies enjoy a warm, bonding, and emotional relationship with their mothers. Finally, breast milk is convenient – it's sterile, needs no preparation, and it's free.

⭐ did you know ...

that breastfeeding has benefits for you too? Women who breastfeed reduce their risk of developing breast, uterine, and ovarian cancers – by as much as 25 per cent for breast cancer. The risk of osteo-porosis and rheumatoid arthritis is reduced significantly too. It is also easier to shift pregnancy weight as breastfeeding burns on average 300–500 calories a day.

Q **Should I be demand-feeding my baby?**

A In the early days it's a good idea to feed as often as your baby wants, simply because your body has to adjust the amount of milk produced to ensure that your baby gets what he needs. After a few weeks, you can choose to continue to feed upon demand, or set up a routine. There are benefits for both approaches, and you'll need to decide what works best for you.

Some childcare experts believe that feeding on demand prevents any problems with milk supply, and also encourages emotional security, because you are meeting your baby's needs as and when he needs you to – teaching him trust. It is also now believed that babies who are fed when they are hungry learn to recognise hunger "cues", and develop a habit of eating to these cues, which is an important step in preventing obesity.

Some women, however, prefer to feed babies according to the clock – often every three or four hours. When babies cry between feeds, they are soothed, but not with milk. This can make life easier, knowing when you'll be sitting down for a feed, and when you have a little more time. Some women don't enjoy breastfeeding in public, and this approach means that you can schedule trips between feeds.

There's no reason, however, why you can't adapt things to include a little of both approaches. For example, you may wish to feed on demand throughout the day, and then wake your baby before you go to bed to fill up his tummy, and give you a little more sleep. You may also want to feed before setting out on a long journey, or to fall in with a family routine. That doesn't mean you are ignoring his requests for food, but that you are rescheduling the feeds a little to avoid having to breastfeed at times that are less convenient.

★ **brainy babies**

Breastfed infants develop higher IQs, and have improved brain and nervous system development – to the extent that breastfeeding is considered by many as the fourth trimester. Also, the way babies suck on the breast promotes development of facial structure, enhancing speech.

Q **How will I know if my baby is getting enough milk?**

A This is a concern that plagues many new mums. Unlike the contents of a bottle, breasts do not supply a "set" amount of milk per feed and do, in fact, adapt constantly to provide your baby with exactly the right amount she needs, according to her demands. There is an element of trust necessary here – believing that your baby is getting what she needs. If your baby is a healthy colour, putting on weight, alert and looking around when she is awake, and has regular wet and dirty nappies, she'll be getting enough. If, after losing a little weight in the first few days, which is entirely normal, your baby puts on weight slowly but surely, all is well. Breastfed babies do tend to gain weight more slowly than their bottle-fed peers, but this is simply a natural process. A health visitor will plot your baby's growth on centile charts in her Child Health Record book (see page 34) – talk to her if you're worried.

Q Will it confuse my baby to have a bottle from time to time?

A Many breastfeeding experts believe that offering a bottle will cause "nipple confusion", mainly because different types of sucking are involved. Sucking from a bottle requires less effort from babies, and they can quite easily become accustomed to getting milk more quickly and efficiently. However, if you can establish a successful pattern of breastfeeding over the first six weeks, your baby will develop the skills he needs to continue, and shouldn't find it too daunting to switch back and forth. In order to keep up the supply, which is based on your baby's demands, it's a good idea to avoid supplementing with formula milk too often.

Q Is it OK to drink a little alcohol if I'm breastfeeding?

A Alcohol enters your milk in much the same way that it does your bloodstream. Within about 20 minutes of drinking, it will appear in your milk. If you are feeling tipsy, you can expect your baby to feel pretty much the same. If you do want a couple of drinks, it's best to have them after you've breastfed, giving your body a chance to clear the alcohol before the next feed. No more than one or two units a week is recommended for breastfeeding mums.

Q Is it necessary to feed from both breasts during every feed?

A The most important thing is to ensure that your baby gets both types of milk produced by your breasts – the thirst-quenching foremilk, and the more calorific and nutritious hind milk. If your baby flits from one breast to the other, without emptying either, she may not be getting enough of the latter. In the early weeks, before the demand for your milk has been established by your baby, your breasts will overproduce quite substantially. A little baby may well be full after emptying the contents of one breast, in which case, it's fine to stop. However, do move her on to the other breast for your next feed, to avoid becoming engorged, and to ensure that your body begins to make the correct amount of milk to meet your baby's needs. Within a few weeks you should be producing the right amount for your baby, and she will be able to manage both breasts in a sitting.

Q How long should my baby feed on each breast?

A It's obviously difficult to work out whether your baby has actually managed to get both fore- and hind milk, because you can't see what is going on. A good feed normally lasts about 20 to 30 minutes. If he's "snacking", falling asleep on the breast, or losing concentration and looking around instead, he probably isn't getting all of what he needs. It may well be that he isn't particularly hungry, and you'll be better off trying again later. If you are demand breastfeeding, which means feeding your baby when he is hungry rather than to a set schedule (see page 13), you might need to urge him to finish a feed properly, or return to the same breast until he has emptied it.

Q If there are allergies in my family, is it advisable to breastfeed?

A Unfortunately, if there is allergy (such as asthma, eczema, hayfever or food allergies) in the family, the likelihood of a baby being "atopic" (the inherited predisposition to allergies) is very high. A huge amount of research has looked at ways of minimizing the potential for "high risk" babies to develop allergies in later life, but very few factors have been shown to make any difference at all. However, there is good evidence that exclusive breastfeeding can help. Current advice is to aim to breastfeed exclusively for six months, although it seems that it is the first four months that have the biggest impact in preventing food allergies and eczema. If there is a strong family history of allergy and you aren't able to breastfeed exclusively for this long, talk to your GP, who may recommend that you try a special hypoallergenic milk formula.

Q Should I wake my baby for a late night feed before I go to bed?

A Personally, I think it's OK to wake your baby. If you don't get much rest, you may find it hard to be a good mother. I think there is more chance of your baby starting to sleep through to a civilized hour if woken and fed just before you go to bed.

Q How long will expressed milk last?

A Expressed milk will last for about four hours at room temperature and, if you refrigerate it immediately after expressing, between 24 and 48 hours. If you are taking expressed milk out with you, keep it in a cool bag with ice packs, and it should last 24 hours or so.

★ sterilizing bottles

It's impossible to create a germ-free environment for your baby. However, warm milk is a perfect breeding ground for germs, so it's important to sterilize the bottles and teats you use for expressed milk. In the first year, your baby will be at her most vulnerable to germs, and carefully washing bottles will not be enough.

Q Can I continue to breastfeed when I return to work?

A If you have access to a breast pump at work, it may be possible to breastfeed exclusively (you'll need to refrigerate the milk and keep it at the same, cool, temperature while you transport it home). Before you return to work, you can freeze a supply of milk – it will last about three months. You'll obviously need to top up this supply. If you're able to feed your baby before you go to work, immediately upon your return, and perhaps again before bedtime or during the night, it is perfectly possible to breastfeed exclusively.

Some mothers who breastfeed part-time, alongside bottle-feeding, find that their babies are reluctant to go back to the breast. However, if you can manage to offer the same feeds each day – perhaps morning and evening – your baby will get used to the routine. Your breasts will also begin to produce milk at the appropriate time.

a new mum's diet

As a new mum, you'll need to make sure that you get plenty of fresh, wholesome food to **keep your energy levels high**. Eating well also helps to ensure that your breastfed baby will have a constant supply of good-quality milk to **keep him healthy and satisfied**.

Q How many calories do I need when I'm breastfeeding?

A Most women need at least 2, 200 calories per day to maintain a supply of good-quality milk, but if you are active, over- or underweight, your needs may be different. Exclusive breastfeeding burns around 300–500 calories per day, and in most cases these need to be replaced. But listen to your body – some days you may need to eat more.

Q Is it OK to diet while breastfeeding?

A This is never a good idea; you need a balanced diet and adequate calories to produce enough good-quality milk for your baby. Also, toxins are stored in fat cells in your body, and when you diet, these are released into your bloodstream and into your milk, eventually reaching your baby. While breastfeeding, you can lose weight healthily (about 2kg/5lb a month) by eating plenty of fresh, whole foods and giving up refined goodies.

Q Which foods should I try to include in my diet while breastfeeding and why?

A A balanced diet will help to ensure that your baby gets the nutrients she needs from your milk, and that you stay healthy, relaxed, and full of energy.

Aim for a diet that is high in unrefined carbohydrates (wholegrain breads, pastas, cereals, brown rice, and grains), which will provide you with sustainable energy and fibre to encourage healthy digestion. Pulses, such as beans, peas, and chickpeas, are an excellent source of healthy unrefined carbs, fibre, vitamins, minerals, and protein. Lentils and chickpeas, in particular, are rich in iron, which can be low in breastfeeding mums. You'll also find iron in dried fruit, fish, and leafy greens, but red meat has the best and most easily absorbed form. Essential fatty acids, found in oily fish, nuts, and seeds, encourage optimum health for you, but they'll also help to ensure that your baby grows and develops properly – in particular, her brain and nervous system. Fresh vegetables and fruit are essential for the vitamins, minerals, and fibre they offer. Finally, aim for four servings of calcium – found in dairy produce, soya, and leafy greens – and three or four servings of protein a day (in lean meats, fish, pulses, eggs, seeds, nuts, and soya).

Q Are there any foods I should avoid while breastfeeding?

A Breast milk is a sweet, nutritious food that takes on the flavours of the foods you are eating, giving your baby her first tastes of food. There are no foods that need to be avoided, but keep an eye out for those that may cause her discomfort. If she appears to be uncomfortable after feeds, crying, vomiting, drawing her knees up to her chest, or experiencing "wind", it may well be that something you have eaten doesn't agree with her. Removing the offending food should make a difference instantly.

Many believe that the foods in a breastfeeding mum's diet can cause colic. Although no-one is exactly sure what causes colic, as the symptoms and causes differ between babies, lots of mums swear by cutting out the "wind-producing" foods, such as cabbage, onions, garlic, and Brussels sprouts.

All studies suggest that what you eat while breastfeeding makes no difference to later allergic disease, including food allergies. However, official advice in the UK and US is that mothers may wish to avoid peanuts during pregnancy and breast-feeding, and to avoid giving infants peanuts for the first three years of their life. This remains contentious and is under review.

Q I find breastfeeding very draining; is there something that I should be eating to lift my energy levels?

A Look at the type of carbohydrates you are eating. If they are mostly "quick-release", you'll experience a surge of energy, followed by a slump that will leave you feeling weary and drained. So go for slow-release carbs, such as wholegrains, pulses, seeds, nuts, and dried fruit, and if you do have unrefined foods in your diet, such as white rice, bread or pasta, cakes, and biscuits, eat them with a little protein to slow down their transit into your blood stream. An egg on white toast, or some cheese on pasta, can make all the difference. Make sure you are getting plenty of iron too. Iron-deficiency anaemia is common in pregnancy and during the postnatal period, and can leave you feeling exhausted. It can help to drink a little fruit juice with iron-rich foods, to encourage their absorption. If all else fails, see your doctor.

★ did you know...

that when you're breastfeeding you need to make sure you drink between 2.5 and 3 litres (4 ½–5 pints), or 8 to 12 glasses of fluids a day? Breastfeeding requires a lot of liquid and if you become dehydrated you'll feel tired and probably irritable or tearful too. It's a good idea to have some water or fresh fruit juice by your side before you settle down to breastfeed. See my refreshing Infused water recipes on page 27 to help quench your thirst.

PREPARATION TIME 10 MINUTES | COOKING TIME 13–17 MINUTES | SERVES 2 ADULTS

beef, mushroom, and spinach stir-fry

Here is a recipe to **boost your iron levels.** Beef and spinach are both high in iron and make a quick and tasty stir-fry. If you put the rice or pasta on to cook before you start stir-frying, dinner will be **on the table in less than 30 minutes.**

2 tbsp sunflower oil

1 onion, halved and thinly sliced

1 garlic clove, crushed

175g (6oz) chestnut mushrooms, thinly sliced

225g (8oz) fillet or sirloin steak, trimmed and cut in thin strips

85g (3oz) baby spinach leaves, washed and dried

150ml (5fl oz) beef stock

1 tbsp oyster sauce

1 tsp soft light brown sugar

1 tsp cornflour

2 tsp water

1 tbsp soy sauce or to taste

To serve

115g (4oz) rice or fusilli pasta, cooked according to packet directions

1 spring onion, shredded (optional)

1 Heat half the oil in a wok or large frying pan, add the onion, and stir-fry for 4–5 minutes until starting to brown. Add the garlic and mushrooms to the wok and stir-fry for another 4–5 minutes until the mushrooms have cooked through and are turning golden at the edges. Spoon the mushrooms and onions into a bowl and set aside.

2 Heat the remaining oil in the wok. Add the steak and stir-fry for 2–3 minutes until browned. Add the spinach and cook for 1–2 minutes until it has wilted, then return the cooked mushrooms and onions to the wok. Add the stock, oyster sauce, sugar, and cornflour blended with the water. Bring to the boil, stirring constantly. Simmer for 1–2 minutes until the sauce has thickened.

3 Add the soy sauce, then taste and add a little more, if you like. Serve spooned over rice or pasta, garnished with the spring onion, if using.

PREPARATION TIME 10 MINUTES PLUS CHILLING | COOKING TIME 30–35 MINUTES | SERVES 2–4 ADULTS

chicken, avocado, and brown rice salad

Eating a combination of protein and whole grains at mealtimes is **a good way to satisfy hunger pangs** and boost energy levels. I love the nuttiness of brown rice in this salad, but you could also use the **wonderful quinoa grain** from Peru. Cook according to the packet instructions.

2 litres (3½ pints) vegetable stock

225g (8oz) brown rice

4 tbsp olive oil

2 tbsp lemon juice

Salt and pepper

1 bunch of spring onions, thinly sliced

55g (2oz) pine nuts, toasted

Handful of fresh coriander leaves, roughly chopped

1 avocado, skin and stone removed, then thinly sliced

2 cooked chicken breasts, thinly sliced

1 Bring the stock to the boil in a large saucepan. Add the rice and stir. Bring back to the boil, then reduce the heat, cover, and cook for 30–35 minutes until the rice is tender and has absorbed all the liquid. Cool and chill until needed (the rice can be cooked up to 24 hours in advance).

2 When ready to serve, whisk together the olive oil and lemon juice with salt and pepper to taste. Stir this dressing into the rice together with the spring onions, pine nuts, and coriander. Top the salad with the avocado and chicken, and serve.

PREPARATION TIME 10 MINUTES | COOKING TIME 9 MINUTES | SERVES 4 ADULTS

annabel's salmon stir-fry with noodles

It's good to eat oily fish like salmon when you are breastfeeding as the **essential fatty acids** are very important for your baby's brain development. In this quick and easy stir-fry, **the vegetables are lightly cooked** to preserve their nutrients, and you can vary them to your own likes and dislikes.

2 tbsp sunflower oil

1 carrot, cut into matchsticks

1 bunch of spring onions, cut diagonally in short lengths

125g (4½oz) broccoli, cut in tiny florets

125g (4½oz) baby sweetcorn, cut in chunks

125g (4½oz) sugar snap peas

450g (1lb) salmon fillet, skinned and cut into 2cm (¾in) cubes

385g (13½oz) pack straight-to-wok noodles

Sauce

2 tbsp plum sauce

2 tbsp hoisin sauce

4 tbsp soy sauce

4 tbsp sake or dry sherry

1tsp toasted sesame oil

1 Mix together the sauce ingredients and set aside.

2 Heat the sunflower oil in a wok or large frying pan. Stir-fry the carrot, spring onions, and broccoli for 2 minutes. Add the sweetcorn and sugarsnap peas and stir-fry for a further 3 minutes.

3 Add the salmon and stir-fry until it it cooked through, about 2 minutes. Add the noodles. Pour over the sauce, toss gently for about 2 minutes until everything is coated in the sauce and the noodles are hot through. Serve in warm bowls.

breastfeeding problems

It can be frustrating to find that choosing to breastfeed isn't always the easiest option, when niggling problems raise their heads. The good news is that almost **all problems can be resolved**, and after the first few weeks you'll find that you settle into a comfortable, **pleasurable routine** with your new baby.

Q **I find I simply don't have enough milk at some points during the day. What do you recommend?**

A It can take some time for your milk to become established, and for "supply and demand" to kick in. Continue to allow your baby to suckle, even if there doesn't seem to be much milk coming out. This will stimulate your body to produce more milk to meet your baby's demands. It may take a day or so for the milk supply to adjust to your baby's needs, and the only way to do this is to continue to try to feed her when she is hungry. Make

sure that you are relaxed when you feed her. If you are tired and anxious, it might seem as though there is no milk, or not enough. In reality, however, even if your breasts do not feel full to bursting, there will be plenty there for your baby.

Take some time to rest, and even retire to bed with your baby for a day or two, to divert your energy towards making milk. Most new mums can do with a break, and once you've got your supply re-established, you'll feel much better.

Make sure, too, that you are getting enough to eat. You need plenty of energy to produce milk, and an inadequate diet can most definitely affect your milk supply. Eat three good meals a day, with plenty of healthy snacks in between, such as wholemeal toast, fresh fruit, cheese, seeds, and nuts (see pages 16–17 for advice on your breastfeeding diet).

⭐ **did you know ...**

that it's perfectly normal for your baby to become distracted while feeding? Even hungry babies can lose interest. Try to find a peaceful place to feed and talk to your baby quietly, so that he concentrates on you rather than what is going on around him. If he starts to come off and on, take him off the breast and try again later. He'll soon realize that feeding time is not playtime!

Q My nipples are sore and chapped, and latching on is becoming very painful; what can I do?

A Breastfeeding in the early days can be quite painful as your nipples adjust to regular feeding. It may be cold comfort, but things do improve over time and the best thing you can do is persevere.

Make sure that your baby is latching on properly. Her mouth needs to be open wide, with her tongue down and forward, and your nipple should be aimed at the roof of her mouth. When she is properly latched on, she should be drawing in all of the nipple, and some breast tissue into her mouth. If you're not sure, ask your midwife, health visitor, or breastfeeding counsellor to watch you feed.

After feeds, express a little of the rich, fatty milk and rub it over your nipple to encourage healing. Between feeds, keep your bra and T-shirt off for short periods, to allow the air to get to your nipples. Try a good emollient cream for sore nipples too.

Q My baby has started refusing my breast; what could be causing this?

A First of all, make sure that you're relaxed and in a quiet spot. If you are feeling fraught or anxious, your baby may respond in kind and become fussy or even reject your breast. Make sure that he's latched on properly, too (see above), as he can become frustrated if he's working hard to feed, and isn't getting much milk. You may find it helps to express a little milk first. Sometimes your milk may flow too quickly, causing your baby to choke and to cry after latching on. If this happens, try using a nipple shield, which slows down the flow. Also, it may be possible that you're eating something that disagrees with your baby (see page 17).

★ teething babies

If your baby is latched on properly, she shouldn't be able to gnaw or bite, but if she's teething she may use your breasts for comfort. Remove her from your breast as soon as she's finished feeding and try rubbing a cold, wet flannel on her gums, or offer her something else to chew on.

Q My baby often goes for hours between feeds, and my breasts become uncomfortable. What should I do?

A Some babies do have an amazing capacity to last for hours between feeds. While it may help to express some milk when your breasts are uncomfortable, you don't want to build up your supply to the extent that you are siphoning off milk and storing it, as well as feeding your baby, as it won't solve the problem in the long-term. Try offering your breast a little more often, even if he doesn't seem to be requesting a feed.

Also, some very young babies have not yet developed the strength to wake up and demand to be fed. Sometimes a premature or ill baby is too small and sleepy to cry, instead focusing on conserving energy for growth and recovery. Waking a baby in this situation to offer the breast is a good idea. If your baby isn't putting on much weight and seems tired and listless, see your doctor or health visitor.

Q My baby still seems hungry after feeds; how do I know that I am producing enough milk?

A If your baby is growing and putting on weight normally, has at least six wet nappies a day, as well as regular bowel movements, is alert when she is awake, but also sleeps well, she will be getting plenty of milk.

Sometimes babies have growth spurts that make them hungrier for short periods of time; these often occur around three weeks, six weeks, three months, and six months. You will need to feed her more frequently during these periods, to build up your milk supply to meet the new demands. It normally takes only 24 to 48 hours for this to happen, so don't panic.

Sometimes babies vomit after feeding, leaving them very hungry. If your baby spits up more than a tablespoon or so of milk after feeds, pay a visit to your doctor to establish the cause. (See pages 36–39 for advice on your baby's health).

Around the four or five month mark, your baby may seem to need more and more milk and may appear less satisfied after feeds. This may be a sign that she is almost ready to start some solid foods. (See pages 40–41 for advice on when to begin weaning your baby).

In most cases, however, you simply need to feed your growing baby more often until things settle down.

Q My baby wakes continually throughout the night for feeds, and I'm becoming exhausted; what can I do?

A First of all, make sure that he is getting plenty of milk during the day, at regular intervals. Babies who develop the habit of snacking tend to wake more frequently than those who have good feeds every three hours or so, as their bodies have not become adjusted to increasing gaps between feeds. If your baby does wake up at night, get him up, change his nappy, and settle him down for a good, long feed. While it does mean that you will have to wake up properly, it's worth considering – he'll go for longer the next time and he'll soon get used to one good feed. If he wakes again, try to settle him without a feed, and he'll soon realize that waking and calling for you isn't going to get him another one.

Q My baby constantly falls asleep while feeding; should I wake her up?

A Babies often fall asleep at the breast, because they are comfortable and deeply relaxed. It's perfectly acceptable to encourage this, but only if they are getting a good feed before they drift off. If your baby is getting only a little drink before she falls asleep, she is likely to wake soon, demanding more – a process that can go on all day and night! It's best to gently nudge her, and switch positions, to encourage her to keep suckling. Sit her up and talk to her, and when she's awake again, put her back on the breast. My mother tells me that she used to tickle my feet to keep me awake. Also try to avoid "big feeds" when she is very tired.

Q I have a real problem with leaking; could I be making too much milk?

A Leaking seems to be a problem that occurs mainly in the first weeks of breastfeeding. Before your supply has been "matched" to your baby's needs, you may produce more milk than your baby needs, causing your breasts to leak and even spurt milk. Try feeding your baby before your breasts become too full. Even if he takes only a little, it can help to ease the flow. Over time, your breasts will respond to your baby's needs, and become less full. If your baby is ill, or if he has slept longer than usual, you may experience very full, painful, leaking breasts. Try expressing a little milk, and put it in the freezer for a later date. Sometimes breasts leak when your let-down reflex suddenly and unexpectedly kicks in. You may hear your baby – or even another baby – cry, which gets things started. Try crossing your arms across your breasts and hold them firmly for a few minutes, to stop the flow, and keep a supply of breast pads to hand.

Q I don't enjoy breastfeeding at all and want to give it up, but I feel incredibly guilty. Does it matter that much?

A Breastfeeding should be a pleasurable experience for both mum and baby, and if you don't enjoy it, it can become negative for you both. Breastfeeding for even a short time gives your baby the best start in life, and you should feel proud that you have managed to give her that. Sometimes it simply doesn't work out, and there are a wide range of good formulas on the market that will ensure your baby gets exactly what she needs. Try not to feel guilty – you can make bottle-feeding sessions warm, nurturing, and positive (see page 30).

Q I would like to stop breastfeeding, but my baby refuses a bottle. What do you recommend?

A First of all, experiment with some different bottle teats. Some of the flatter ones are more similar to the nipple, and he may find this less offensive. Start by offering him expressed milk in a bottle, which he'll find familiar and less distressing. Try dropping one feed at a time, and offering the bottle when you know he'll be hungry – perhaps first thing in the morning. It can sometimes help to have someone else offer the bottle, because if he's near to you, and can smell your milk, he may hold out for the real thing. Make sure the bottle-feeding experience is cosy and nurturing (see page 30). It can be difficult, but persevere, and he'll get there. If he's hungry, he'll eventually give in, and one or two successful bottle feeds will make things much easier in future.

★ breastfeeding to sleep

Many babies seek the breast when they are sleepy because it's comforting and familiar. There is nothing wrong with breastfeeding a baby to sleep. You don't want her to become dependent on you feeding her to fall asleep, though. Begin the transition to settling her without milk when you're both ready.

PREPARATION TIME 5 MINUTES PLUS CHILLING | MAKES 1.5 LITRES (2¾ PINTS)

infused waters

It is important to **drink plenty of fluids** when breastfeeding, but try to avoid sugar-filled fizzy drinks and caffeine. Posh health spas serve infused waters, **which are refreshing**, and a lot more interesting than plain water. Why not make your own, and refrigerate until needed?

lime, cucumber, and mint

1 lime, thinly sliced

7.5cm (3in) piece cucumber, peeled, halved lengthways, and finely sliced

2 large sprigs of fresh mint

1.5 litres (2¾ pints) water

1 Put the lime, cucumber, mint, and water in a large jug (or divide between two smaller jugs).

2 Cover and chill overnight. Stir before serving.

citrus refresher

1 lemon, thinly sliced

1 lime, thinly sliced

1 orange, thinly sliced

1.5 litres (2¾ pints) water

1 Put the sliced fruit and water in a large jug (or divide between two smaller jugs).

2 Cover and chill overnight. Stir before serving.

PREPARATION TIME 5 MINUTES | COOKING TIME 4–5 MINUTES | SERVES 1 ADULT

chicken quesadilla

Quesadillas are quick and tasty, perfect **when you are hungry** and tired, and want an **end-of-the-day snack** without any fuss.

2 flour tortillas (wraps)

2 tbsp salsa

55g (2oz) cooked chicken breast, shredded

30g (1oz) Cheddar cheese, grated

To serve

1 tbsp soured cream (optional)

2 tbsp guacamole or a few avocado slices (optional)

1 Place a large, non-stick frying pan over a medium heat to warm up.

2 Put one tortilla on a plate and spread over the salsa. Scatter the chicken and cheese evenly over the tortilla, and top with the second tortilla. Slide into the hot frying pan and lower the heat slightly. Cook for about 2 minutes or until the underside is toasted, pressing the quesadilla down lightly with a fish slice or spatula.

3 Using your hand to steady the top, carefully flip over the quesadilla with a fish slice or spatula. Cook for a further 2–3 minutes until the second side is toasted, pressing down lightly. When the quesadilla is ready, the cheese will have melted and the chicken will be hot through. (If flipping the quesadilla makes you nervous, you can pop the frying pan under a preheated grill to toast the top.)

4 Slide the quesadilla on to a plate and leave to stand for 1–2 minutes, then cut in quarters. Serve with soured cream and guacamole or avocado slices, if you like.

all about bottle-feeding

Not everyone finds it easy or possible to breastfeed, but you can be confident that **formula milk offers your baby** the nutrients that will encourage optimum health and development. Bottle-feeding also gives **dad and other members of the family** a chance to experience the wonders of feeding a new baby.

Q **Is there anything I can do to encourage bonding if I'm bottle-feeding?**

A Making the experience of being fed pleasurable and nurturing is important whether you are breastfeeding or bottle-feeding, and physical comfort is the most important element of this.

Hold your baby close to you and let her know that she's safe and secure in your arms. Keep her pressed close to your chest, so that she can hear your heartbeat, smell you, and feel comforted. Talk quietly to her, or sing, so that she can hear your voice, and be reassured that you are there for her. Look into her eyes, stroke her face, and encourage her to do the same in return. Babies love to be cuddled and held, and skin-to-skin contact is also recommended from time to time, which mimics the breastfeeding experience. A good routine also helps, so your baby knows what to expect and looks forward to this positive experience.

Q **What should I look for in a formula?**

A The truth is that most formulas are pretty much the same. All now contain essential fatty acids (EFAs), which are essential for your baby's healthy growth and development – in particular, the development of her brain and nervous system. Others also offer probiotics, a substance that promotes the growth of good bacteria in your baby's gut.

Like all milks, breast milk contains two types of protein: whey and casein. The balance in breast milk is in favour of whey (70 per cent whey and 30 per cent casein). It is a good idea, therefore, to look for a formula with a similar ratio. Formulas that have more casein tend to be harder for your baby to digest, and are more suited to the older infant.

There may be other claims made on your baby's formula packet, such as additional immune-boosting nutrients, etc; however, it's worth noting that baby formula manufacturing is very, very closely monitored, and nothing can be added without going through rigorous scrutiny by government health authorities. For this reason, there will be little difference between formulas – once one brand has an extra ingredient, the others soon follow suit.

Q Is there any advantage to buying pre-mixed formulas?

A The main advantage to pre-mixed formulas is their convenience. They can be carried with you wherever you go, and used on the spot, with no mixing or preparation. This is particularly useful when travelling, as you may not have the equipment you need to prepare feeds, nor any way to sterilize the implements. Many parents find it useful to use pre-mixed formulas at home, too – mainly because they take the hard work out of bottle-feeding, and there is no concern about the formula being inaccurately measured (see box, below). The disadvantage, however, is that they are expensive.

Q Can I use mineral water when preparing my baby's formula?

A Mineral water is not recommended in the preparation of formula, because it is designed for adults and not babies, and contains (not surprisingly) minerals, including salt, which your baby does not need. There will be the correct balance of minerals in your baby's formula, and adding additional ones in the form of mineral water can upset the balance. Bottled spring water is fine, as it has a lower concentration of minerals.

Q Are there particular types of bottles or teats that are easier for a baby to manage?

A Narrow-necked bottles tend to be more versatile, because they will take most teats designed for this type of bottle. Silicone teats tend to be more expensive, but they are more durable and will last longer. Latex teats can, however, be softer than silicone, which makes it easier for some babies to suck (particularly if they have a weak suck).

Choose a teat that is the right size for the age of your baby, and experiment a little to see if he prefers faster or slow-flow teats. Most babies will finish a bottle in no more than 20 minutes, so if it is taking longer, consider switching to a faster teat. If he's finishing a bottle in less than 10 minutes, switch to a slower one.

I've found that some babies, particularly those who have started out being breastfed, seem to prefer the teats that are shaped more like a nipple, with a wide, flat base, and a "nipple-shaped" centre.

★ **did you know ...**

that it is very important to follow the manufacturer's instructions when making up formula milk? This may seem fiddly at first, but it will soon become second nature. Formula milk is perfectly balanced to ensure that it is easily digestible, and meets your baby's needs. Too much of the powder or liquid can cause your baby to become constipated, or thirsty; too little may mean she isn't getting the nutrition she needs.

Q Is it OK to store bottles of made-up formula milk in the fridge?

A It is recommended that bottles should be made immediately before a feed, rather than prepared in advance and stored in the fridge – for hygiene reasons. It may seem a little over-cautious, but the powder itself is not sterile and there is a small risk that the made-up formula could become contaminated with micro-organisms. Discard any of your baby's half-finished bottles when she has finished feeding. Don't be tempted to reheat them later on, since this can allow harmful bacteria to multiply.

If you are out for the day, use an insulated container to store freshly boiled water and mix up with the formula powder or liquid when you need it. See the tips for travelling on the opposite page.

⭐ the right temperature

Heating formula milk to the correct temperature is important. It should be at body temperature. Check this by shaking a few drops on the inside of your wrist – you shouldn't feel the milk. You can heat your baby's milk in the microwave, but look out for "hot spots" in the milk, which can burn your baby's mouth. Shake it carefully after heating, and do not offer until it has reached body temperature.

Q My baby has had an upset tummy since I changed her formula; should I go back?

A It's probably a good idea to go back to your original formula, which may have a different ratio of casein to whey (see page 30) or simply a different combination of nutrients. Some babies are very sensitive to change, which is why it can be sensible to bring stocks of his usual formula when travelling (see below). If he doesn't improve when you return him to his original formula, it would be a good idea to see your doctor to establish whether or not there is another cause.

Q My baby will only accept a certain formula, which makes it difficult when we travel or run short. What should I do?

A Many babies become very attached to a specific formula, and will be resistant to trying anything new. You can help to prevent this problem by swapping between two similar brands from time to time, to accustom her to different tastes and nutrient balances. You can also purchase a supply of her regular formula in "ready-made" format, to take with you on holiday (see page 30). If you go prepared with plenty of formula, you will hopefully not be caught short. If you do find yourself running out of your baby's favourite formula, try making up a bottle of another brand and mixing it with your baby's usual milk. She may be less resistant if the taste is very similar, and you can eventually eliminate her original formula altogether.

As there's so little difference between formula milks, if you switch between them, your baby will get used to different flavours. After all, breast milk changes flavour all the time.

Q Does my baby need extra water if he is drinking his formula?

A Neither breast- nor bottle-fed babies should need any extra water as milk provides all the fluid they require until six months of age. However, you may occasionally want to offer some cool boiled water if the weather is very hot, he is unsettled between feeds, or he is constipated. However, be careful not to give too much, and to offer it after feeds, as there are no calories in water and it will fill him up, possibly causing his weight gain to suffer.

Q Do I really have to sterilize everything I use to prepare formula?

A It is important to sterilize everything involved in the preparation of your baby's milk. The reason is that even small traces of bacteria on a spoon or jug can multiply and cause sometimes serious health problems for your baby. Your baby's milk contains sugars that will literally feed bacteria, which can breed very quickly, particularly in warm milk.

Q Do I have to use a sterilizer for all the bottles, or will the dishwasher do?

A The dishwasher is fine, as long as the machine is clean, and the other dishes washed alongside are not covered with food debris, which can cling to the bottles and the teats, and attract harmful bacteria once removed from the machine. It's also important to ensure that your machine reaches a temperature of at least 80°C (175°F) or more, which is necessary to kill bacteria and viruses. Rinse the bottles in cooled, previously boiled, water when you take them out, to remove all traces of detergent, and fill the bottles with formula as soon as possible.

Q How can I sterilize my baby's bottles when we are travelling?

A If you have access to a kitchen, microwave sterilizer bags are good for travelling. Also, you can now buy microwavable bottles that can be sterilized in the microwave on their own. You can sterilize bottles and teats in a dishwasher too (see left). Otherwise, the most effective method is to boil them for about 10 minutes in a clean pan (the pan needs to be used exclusively for this purpose), which will remove any potentially harmful germs and bacteria.

You may not always have access to a kitchen or electricity, though, in which case cold-water sterilization, using a non-toxic solution is your best bet. You can purchase fluid or tablets that can be added to water in special sterilizing units or a clean plastic container with a lid. The bottles will need to be soaked, submerged, for about half an hour, and you may wish to rinse them with cool, previously boiled water to remove all traces of the solution, although this isn't necessary. You can leave the bottles in the solution for up to 24 hours, and use them as required. Remember that they can quickly lose their sterility, so try to fill them immediately after they have been treated.

weight worries

It's natural for new parents to be concerned that their baby is growing and developing at the right speed, and that he is getting the right **amount of milk for his needs**. Rest assured that within the first few weeks, your new baby will let you know exactly what he needs, and **you'll soon become alert** to any potential problems.

Q **How can I tell that my baby is growing normally?**

A When your baby is born, you'll be given a growth chart, usually in the back of your baby's record book, on which the healthcare professional will plot her height and weight. The current growth charts are based mainly on bottle-fed infants, but you can ask for a chart designed for breastfed babies if your baby is exclusively breastfed. For the sake of accuracy, it is important to have your baby weighed at her clinic from time to time, to ensure that you have the correct data.

From birth, your baby's height and weight can be plotted on the chart, which is broken up into "centiles". The centile charts work on averages so being on the "50th centile" for weight or height means your baby is absolutely average for her age. Similarly, being on the "91st centile" for height indicates that your baby is tall for her age. The idea of plotting these figures is to ensure that your little one remains on much the same line as she grows. So if she was born heavy, she is likely to remain heavy throughout infancy and into childhood, and if she was born smaller than most other babies, she is likely to remain on that line as well. There will always be upwards and downwards blips, and it's important not to worry too much about these, as they represent normal growth patterns. What you are looking for is a fairly regular picture over time. In the short-term, if your baby is alert, putting on weight, sleeping well, and looks well and content, she will be growing properly and there is no need for concern.

Q **My baby was small at birth and is still slight for his height; should I be worried?**

A If your baby is on roughly the same centile line that he was when he was born, there is absolutely no need for concern. Some children (and adults) are smaller and slighter than others, and are perfectly healthy. He may have a significant growth spurt later in childhood, which may bring him to a more average height and weight for his age, or he may remain small. If he's healthy and well, and growing normally, there is nothing to worry about.

★ **did you know...**

that it's very important to weigh your baby on the same scale, with the same clothing (or no clothing), each time, in order to be sure that you get an accurate result? Scales can vary enormously, and you don't want to be sent into a panic that your baby has suddenly "gained" or "lost" a large amount of weight. You can expect your baby to put on between 100g (3½oz) and 225g (8oz) a week in his first few months.

Q My baby seems hungry even though I'm giving her the recommended number of feeds. Is it OK to offer more?

A All babies have different needs, and formula manufacturers base their instructions upon the average baby. The best advice is to offer about 120–150ml (4–5fl oz) of milk per kg (2lb 3oz) of body weight during each 24-hour period while your baby is below 5kg (11lb). If your baby still seems hungry, try offering an extra 30–60ml (1–2fl oz) during each feed, to see if that makes a difference. If your baby's weight is above 5kg (11lb), she will need 100–120ml (3⅓–4 fl oz) per kg (2lb 3oz) of body weight.

It is important to follow your baby's hunger and satiety patterns. If babies demand more, they often need more. Your baby may be experiencing a growth spurt (see page 24) or she may be trying to tell you that she is ready for solids (see page 40).

Sometimes very hungry babies will need a formula with more casein than whey. These take longer to digest, helping babies to feel fuller for longer.

Q Is it possible to overfeed my baby?

A It is possible to overfeed a bottlefed baby, and this can lead to vomiting, diarrhoea, and excess weight gain. It is therefore important to interpret your baby's cues and not just feed whenever he feels unsettled. It is difficult to feed a breastfed baby too much, as you will make just the right amount of milk that he needs.

Newborns often have six to eight feeds per day, dropping to four or five by around seven months. The amount you offer should be based on your baby's weight (see left), and he should be satisfied by the time he finishes his bottle. There should always be a little milk left in the bottle at the end of each feed, so you can be sure he has stopped feeding because he has had enough milk, rather than because there was no more available. If you find your baby is always hungry, and putting on weight too quickly, talk to your doctor or health visitor. It may be that he's ready to begin weaning (see page 40).

your new baby's health

Illness in a new baby can be **a daunting and worrying time**, and little ones can lose weight quickly when they are unwell. The most **important thing is not to panic**, and to follow your instincts. Your doctor or health visitor will be a source of practical, reassuring advice, so **be sure to talk to them** about any worries you may have.

Q **My baby often vomits after feeds; is this normal?**

A Possetting, which means regurgitating a small amount of milk after feeds, is normal. In most cases it is caused when bubbles of air become trapped while feeding. Normal winding will usually bring these up, but a small amount of milk may reappear as well. In some cases, it may reappear quickly, sometimes through your baby's nose.

You can help prevent possetting by handling your baby gently after a feed, particularly when winding her; turning her upright immediately after a feed; providing smaller, more regular feeds, rather than filling her tummy to brimming; keeping your baby at an upright angle while feeding her; and, if she falls asleep soon after the feed, raising the head of her cot slightly by placing a folded blanket underneath her mattress, to lift her to a slight angle (about 20°).

If you are breastfeeding, you can also try reducing wind-producing foods in your diet, such as cabbage, beans, lentils, broccoli, and onions.

Bottlefeeding? Try to avoid overfeeding by letting her have a break before the bottle is finished, and wind her about halfway through the bottle.

Q **What is gastric reflux?**

A Gastric reflux is a more severe form of possetting, but it has a physiological cause. It is usually the result of a weak valve at the top of your baby's tummy, which allows the feed, along with gastric juices, to come back up, causing vomiting and a burning sensation, similar to heartburn. If your baby continually brings up her feed, seems in pain during feeding, is taking only small amounts of milk, and cries excessively, he may have reflux.

In most cases, it resolves itself during weaning and doesn't harm your baby. However, see a doctor for a diagnosis and treatment. In more severe cases, a pre-thickened formula milk or antacid may be given. Elevate your baby's bed slightly (see left) to help ease discomfort, and refer to the other tips for easing possetting, too. It may also help to offer solids a little earlier (see pages 40–41); it's best to discuss this with your doctor.

Q What should I do if my baby has a diarrhoea and vomiting virus?

A The best thing to do is to continue with her normal milk, offering feeds little and often, and if this continues beyond two days, take her to the doctor. It's very easy for small babies to become dehydrated, which can become a serious problem if it is not treated. Signs of dehydration include a sunken fontanelle (the soft spot on your baby's head); listlessness; sunken eyes; dry mouth, eyes, and lips; dark-coloured urine; and much fewer wet nappies (fewer than six per day).

Once diarrhoea and vomiting start, monitor your baby for signs of dehydration and ensure that you keep up her milk intake. Breastfed babies will need increased feeds, and possibly some additional oral rehydration solution. Bottle-fed babies are likely to need 24 hours on oral rehydration solution, with a little formula in between, although it might be necessary to continue to offer water and oral rehydration solution for a further few days. The most important thing is to keep your baby hydrated, and any fluid, such as water, will do.

If the diarrhoea and vomiting are not accompanied by a fever, and do not seem to be linked to gastroenteritis, it's worth seeing your doctor to establish if your baby is allergic to milk (see page 38 for more information).

Furthermore, many little ones develop lactose intolerance after a tummy bug. This is because they lose the enzyme to digest lactose. In this case, your doctor will suggest switching your baby to a lactose-free formula for a short period (around four to six weeks in most cases), after which your baby will be able to tolerate her normal formula milk again.

Q My sick baby doesn't seem interested in her regular milk; what should I do?

A Just like adults, babies who are unwell may not feel hungry, and will refuse feeds. However, because babies can become dehydrated so easily, it is very important to offer plenty of water. If your baby does become dehydrated (see left for symptoms), it may be necessary to offer an oral rehydration solution, and in this situation, you should always pay a visit to your doctor. Do continue to offer him regular feeds, but don't be tempted to dilute his regular milk, which is carefully blended to ensure the right balance of nutrients and fluid. It's particularly important that you continue to offer your baby feeds if you are breastfeeding, as your milk contains antibodies that will help him to fight any infection.

★ feed a fever?

If your baby has a fever, continue breast or bottle-feeding as normal, and if she seems resistant, offer her more frequent, smaller feeds. Any baby under the age of six months with a fever should be seen by a doctor. If your baby is older than this, use your judgement, and keep a close eye on her. If she is listless and failing to take her feeds, you should call a doctor straight away.

⭐ **allergy worry**

It is important to note that the symptoms associated with allergies (see right) commonly occur during infancy, and allergy is only one explanation. Also, although allergies are increasingly common, only a small proportion of the population are affected by food allergies (approximately 6–8 per cent of infants and 3.7 per cent of adults in the UK and US). There is no need to worry unduly that your baby will suffer from allergies unless your family has a history of allergy (including hayfever, asthma, eczema, or food allergies) or your baby suffers from eczema. However, if you are concerned that your baby has an allergy, or you're worried about your baby's health in any way, speak to your doctor or health visitor.

Q Could my baby's colic be the result of the formula I'm giving him?

A Colic is one sign that your baby may not be tolerating the formula you give him. You could try switching brands, although most are identical, and this may not make a difference.

If the problem is recurrent, and associated with other symptoms (see right), or if your baby seems very distressed or unwell after feeds, see your doctor, who may prescribe anti-reflux medication or, if unsuccsessful, a hydrolyzed formula.

Q If my baby seems uncomfortable after a feed, could she have food allergies?

A A baby may seem uncomfortable after a feed for a variety of reasons, and allergy is only one of them. Food allergies are more common in families with a history of allergies and babies with eczema. A sign of allergy in babies is discomfort, as well as rashes on her face or body, and even eczema. Diarrhoea, vomiting, colic, distress and constant crying, hives, and breathing difficulties are also possible signs that something in her milk is not agreeing with her. It's very important to take these symptoms seriously– talk to your doctor if you're concerned (and in the case of breathing difficulties, call for an ambulance immediately). See page 58 for more information on how allergies are diagnosed.

Q My baby has persistent diarrhoea – should I change his formula?

A If your baby has recurrent diarrhoea or vomiting, and doesn't seem to be thriving on the formula you have offered, it's most certainly worth looking at the potential causes.

If you suspect that your baby's formula is making him ill, see your doctor immediately. If a milk allergy is diagnosed, in most cases a hydrolyzed formula will be offered. This contains all of the nutrients your baby needs for normal growth and development, and is perfectly safe. They are not very pleasant-tasting, however. Babies who don't know any different accept the taste, but it can be difficult to introduce if your baby is used to normal formula.

Be aware that goat's, rice, oat, pea, and nut milk are not recommended for babies, and soya milk should not be introduced before six months.

Q My baby seems to be reacting to my breast milk. Should I switch to formula?

A Breast milk is still the very best nutrition for your baby. Whether your baby is truly allergic, or simply experiencing a temporary reaction to certain foods in your diet, making changes to what you eat, with the help of a dietitian, can make a difference. Remember, too, that many babies are fussy in the first few months, regardless of what you are eating. Unless your baby experiences other symptoms, such as vomiting or diarrhoea (see left), chances are she'll outgrow this and continue to breastfeed happily.

Q My baby has a cold and is having trouble feeding because he can't breathe through his nose – what should I do?

A It can be very difficult for babies to feed when their nasal passages are blocked, and they may end up going on and off the bottle or breast with a series of gasps for air. Place a few drops of eucalyptus oil in a bowl of hot water near the feeding chair, to open his airways, or squirt a little saline solution into his nose before feeding. Holding him upright can help, and, if all else fails, buy an aspirator – to suck the mucus from his nostrils.

Q Is it possible to diagnose food allergies this early?

A Even young babies can have food allergies diagnosed, but it's important to remember that not all symptoms are the result of allergies. In some cases, your baby may simply be irritated by something you are eating, and become temporarily fussy. For example, onions, cauliflower, and broccoli can cause your baby to experience gas, and other foods such as chocolate may cause your baby to have diarrhoea.

On rare occasions, newborns can be allergic to foods passing through their mothers' breast milk – for example cow's milk and eggs. The reaction in this instance tends to be eczema flare-ups or an upset tummy, rather than wheezing or hives.

In other cases, make a note of any symptoms that appear after feeding your baby (see pages 57–58), and see your doctor to work out how best to eliminate them.

★ **did you know ...**

that an increasing number of little ones are showing signs of vitamin D deficiency? Vitamin D is important for the formation of healthy bones and immunity. The best way to ensure your baby has adequate levels is to get him out in the sunshine for a few minutes each day. Some dark-skinned babies in northern climates may require a little extra vitamin D, in the form of vitamin drops, because their darker skin makes it harder for them to absorb the sun's rays.

time for the first taste?

The first months of your baby's life may fly by, and as **the gaps between feeds lengthen**, and he becomes more alert and expends more energy, you may find that he is **showing signs of being ready** for solid food. Let your baby take the lead.

Q My four-month-old seems hungry all the time – could she be ready to begin solids?

A Currently the most common recommendation for weaning age comes from the World Health Organization (WHO), which suggests waiting until six months of age to introduce solids. We know, however, that babies' digestive and immune systems can tolerate food a little earlier (from around 17 weeks of age), and so the exact timing is really dependent on your baby; every baby is different. If your baby is demanding feeds more often, shows an interest in the food you are eating (for example reaching out for food on your plate), and is "mouthing" (chewing on her knuckles or putting her fingers in her mouth), it is likely that she's ready. Speak to your health visitor if you think this is the case. Suitable early weaning foods include vegetables, fruit, and cereals (see page 47 for more advice).

Q Why do experts now recommend waiting until six months to wean?

A All countries, and health experts, have adopted the guidelines from the WHO, which recommends exclusive breastfeeding until six months. This is particularly important in underdeveloped countries, where breast milk is sterile and the safest feeding option, and is also a good safeguard for children who may have a poor weaning diet.

The main reason to wait until six months is that until this time your breast milk will provide your baby with everything he needs to grow and develop; however, after this, breast milk alone provides insufficient essential nutrients, like iron and vitamin D. That's not to say that breast milk has no nutritional value after this time (see page 45), but your baby's growth and development demands more nutrients that need to be provided through weaning foods. Similarly, formula-fed infants also need to be weaned at six months, to supplement nutritional intake. If your baby does show signs that he is ready for solid food a little earlier (see left), it's a good idea to speak to your health visitor about the possibility of introducing some simple foods, as these will ensure normal oral motor skill development in your baby (i.e. sucking and chewing).

Q Will early weaning make my baby more prone to allergies?

A Another argument that is sometimes put forward against weaning babies earlier than six months is based on the notion that early weaning makes babies more prone to allergies. However, this is not true. Most babies' digestive systems can tolerate basic food from around 17 weeks, and there is no evidence that delaying weaning beyond this time prevents allergies in either allergic or non-allergic infants.

Q Does my baby need juice or water alongside her milk feeds?

A Breastfed babies do not need water or juice, as your milk is perfectly balanced, both to quench thirst and to keep her well hydrated. If she has a virus and is struggling to keep down her milk, you may need to offer water or oral rehydration solution to ensure that she does not become dehydrated (see page 37), although the best advice is to continue breastfeeding, both to ensure she gets enough fluids, and to take advantage of the antibodies that your breast milk offers. Bottle-fed babies may need to have a little water alongside their feeds (see page 33).

Baby juices are not necessary at this age, as your baby will be getting all the nutrients she needs from her milk. If she's thirsty and not interested in water, you could heavily dilute a little baby juice, but you may be making a rod for your own back, as she will be less likely to take plain water later on, if she's used to the sweetness of juice. If she is ill and there is risk of dehydration, however, any fluids, such as heavily diluted juice, water, and oral rehydration solution are appropriate.

Q My baby keeps reaching out for other people's food. Should I let him taste?

A Once again, from around five months onwards, small tastes of food are acceptable. Be aware, however, that your baby won't have developed the ability to chew, and won't for some time, so anything offered should be soft and, ideally, puréed. Remember to keep to foods that are suitable for your baby's age (see pages 47 and 61). Steer away from foods that contain flavourings, colourings, and sweeteners, and avoid anything with sugar and salt, as you'll want to encourage your little one to develop a taste for the natural sweetness of foods such as fruit and vegetables, before a sweet tooth can be established.

★ mastering a cup

Most babies drink from a cup at around four months, although you will have to hold it to his mouth and encourage him to sip. He should be able to do this himself at around six months, although some little ones may manage it sooner, and others a little later. Don't worry if your baby shows no interest. He should be getting adequate fluids from his milk feeds (and solids – if he's begun weaning). It may be easier to offer all drinks, apart from milk in a cup, to prevent him from developing the habit of taking everything from a bottle.

chapter 2

6–9 months:
ready for food

6–9 months:
what you can expect

Your baby's first spoonfuls are an exciting milestone for both you and your baby. It's only natural to approach weaning with some anxiety – there are lots of things to consider as your baby begins his journey on the road to independence, but it's a process you'll both enjoy.

Q How do I know if my baby is ready for solid foods?

A Your baby will start to show some interest in what you are eating, and perhaps reach out to taste it himself. He will probably be hungrier than usual, often unsatisfied after his normal milk feed, and possibly waking in the night for an extra feed, when he has previously slept through. He should be "mouthing" too – putting his fingers in his mouth or chewing on his knuckles.

It's worth noting that a growth spurt commonly occurs between three and four months of age, which may cause him to wake more frequently at night, and perhaps feed much more frequently (sometimes appearing to be non-stop!). This growth spurt accounts for his hunger, so don't assume he's ready for solids just yet!

Q Do I still need to breastfeed when I begin weaning?

A Your baby will need formula or breast milk until she is at least 12 months, when her diet is varied enough to offer the correct balance of nutrients. Weaning foods offer first tastes rather than proper nutrition, and as she gradually eats more, her milk feeds will be replaced by proper meals. Don't be tempted to give up the milk, though. Breastfeed as usual, or, if you are bottle-feeding, remember that she will need at least 500–600ml (about 1 pint) per day. If less than this is consumed, it's worth discussing with a doctor or health visitor, as she may need extra vitamins. Give her a milk feed first thing in the morning and at bedtime, and other milk feeds during the day. The timing will depend on the stage of weaning, but you should try to give milk feeds after meals and limit the amount of milk between meals.

Q Why should I make homemade purées for my baby?

A The healthiest baby foods are the ones you make yourself. You can be sure of using the best-quality ingredients with no thickeners or additives, including salt or sugar. The ingredients of most commercial baby foods are heated to a very high temperature and then cooled, to sterliize them – a process that destroys some nutrients. By using fresh ingredients, your homemade purées will be that much more nutritious.

Homemade purées taste much better too, and they're a great way to introduce your baby to the delights of fresh, whole foods, with their intrinsic sweetness and flavours. Put some time in now, and you'll reap the benefits later. Giving your baby homemade food will help to make the transition to family food much easier.

★ cheap, healthy food

Would you believe that parents in the UK fork out around £70 million every year on commercially prepared baby food? By making your own, you'll be saving money (even taking into consideration the time it takes for you to make them), and you'll be giving your child a great start in life.

beginning weaning

This time is **an important transition** for you and your baby. Whether she's a slow starter, or instant foodie, you'll both **take pleasure in the process** of mastering self-feeding, introducing new tastes, and **enjoying the world of food**.

Q Can I wait longer than six months to introduce first foods?

A It may be tempting to wait, given that your baby's digestive and immune systems will be that much more mature, but it doesn't help to do so.

For one thing, babies who start later often find it difficult to manage lumps, and may be more reluctant to try new tastes and textures. Also, if you wait to introduce fruit and vegetables, you'll delay moving on to protein-rich foods, such as oily fish, which contain essential fatty acids that are vital for your baby's development. Also, a baby's iron supply, inherited from his mother, runs out at six months, so it's important not to wait too long before introducing iron-rich foods such as red meat and lentils. With regards to food allergies, there is no evidence that delaying the introduction of allergenic foods (such as cow's milk, egg, wheat, fish, and soya) after the six-month mark makes your child less likely to have food allergies.

Q What is the best way to introduce solids to my baby?

A Firstly, don't worry about how much your baby is eating. The idea of first foods is to encourage your baby to experience new tastes and textures, and to get used to the idea of taking something from a spoon and swallowing it. While nutrition is important – meaning, simply, that everything you offer your baby should be fresh and nutritious – it's actually more important that she develops a taste for a variety of different foods.

It's perfectly fine to introduce new foods to your baby each day. If there is a history of allergy in the family (see page 58), you may like to offer a new food every two or three days, so you can watch out for any signs of a reaction. Reactions that can indicate a potential problem include skin rashes, vomiting, diarrhoea, and even breathing difficulties.

To begin with, offer food halfway through a milk feed, so your baby isn't frantically hungry. At first, the purées need to be semi-liquid, and as much like milk in consistency as possible so that they are easy to swallow – add breast milk, formula, or a little water from the bottom of the steamer or saucepan, to thin the purée.

Q What is "baby-led" weaning?

A Baby-led weaning is an interesting concept. The idea is that you miss out the purée stage, and allow your baby to feed herself. It is believed that babies who are weaned in this way are less likely to become fussy eaters, but there is no evidence to support this.

Many feeding difficulties can start when babies make the transition from purées to lumpier foods, to which they are often resistant. Instead, babies are encouraged to chew from the outset, eating what they want from a selection of foods that can be picked up and held (see page 61). Your baby may play with, or suck, the food, but eventually she'll eat more and develop healthy eating habits.

There is, of course, a risk of choking, as babies may bite off a chunk of food that they are then unable to chew and swallow, so you should never leave your baby unattended. Your baby may also choose to eat the same few foods, avoiding foods that don't appeal, unlike when you choose your baby's purées and you're in the driving seat.

Ultimately it's up to you. Personally, I like the idea of introducing different tastes and textures in the form of purées, which babies can easily master and digest. You can then make a gradual transition to lumpier foods and finger foods, over a few weeks.

Q What is the best first weaning food?

A Root vegetables are a good first bet, so consider potatoes, carrots, sweet potatoes, and parsnips.

Baby rice is also a good start, but I prefer to mix it with fruit or vegetable pureés, as it is very bland on its own. At first, mix it with very runny purées, such as pear.

Mashed avocados are sweet and extremely nutritious, and as your baby becomes accustomed to different vegetables, you can start to introduce fruit. Sometimes it's a good idea to blend fruit with vegetables at the outset, as canny babies will work out that fruit is sweeter, and reject their favourite vegetable purées in favour of fruit. Always start a meal with a vegetable purée, or fruit and vegetable blend, and then move on to fruit, so that your baby gets a good balance of vitamins and minerals, and doesn't turn her nose up at the veggies once she's had a taste of the sweeter fruit.

★ did you know ...

that the more tastes to which you introduce your young baby, and the wider the range of combinations, the more likely he is to develop his "palate" and enjoy different foods? Try introducing new foods one a time at the outset, and then, when the food has been successfully introduced, offer a blend. When introducing stronger-tasting flavours, like spinach or broccoli, it is a good idea to mix them with a root vegetable, such as sweet potato or carrot.

Q Is it a good idea to put baby rice or other cereals in my baby's bottle?

A This is a long out-dated practice, and it should not be undertaken. When your baby is ready for solids, these should be offered with a spoon (or as a finger food) and not via a bottle. One of the important elements of weaning is teaching your little one to remove food from a spoon, to chew or "gum" it, and then to swallow. If you offer these first foods in a bottle, your baby will not learn these skills, which are a key part of her developmental process.

Parents may be tempted to offer a little "extra" in their baby's bottle, in the hope that they will get a little more sleep by keeping tummies full; however, food in the bottle can pose a choking hazard.

While it's OK to offer cereal as a first taste, it's better to introduce a variety of nutritious fresh purées as your baby grows. Babies tend to eat pretty well in the first year, so it's a great opportunity to offer as much variety as possible.

★ storing purées

Fresh purées will last 48 hours in the fridge and eight weeks in the freezer. The temperature of your fridge should be 4°C (40°F) and your freezer -18°C (0°F). You shouldn't reheat food more than once and never refreeze foods. It's OK, however, to re-freeze vegetables, such as frozen peas.

Q Do I need special equipment for making purées?

A You don't need much more than a food processor and ice-cube tray, but there are a few things that might make life a little easier.

It's worth buying a multi-layered steamer, as steaming or microwaving is the best way to preserve the nutrients in vegetables, and a multi-layered steamer allows you to cook several vegetables at one time. If you use a microwave, a dish with a valve in the lid, which opens to release steam, is ideal for cooking fish or vegetables. A baby food grinder, which is a hand-turned food mill, can be very useful, especially in the early weeks when you'll be making very smooth purées. It is great for foods with tough skins, such as peas or dried apricots, as it discards the bits that are indigestible. It's also good for potato, as puréeing potato in a food processor tends to break down the starches and produces a sticky, glutinous pulp.

Another useful addition is an electric hand blender. This is ideal for making baby purées, as it can handle very small quantities.

Store purées in an ice-cube tray with a lid, if possible, to keep food covered for maximum freshness. One that is flexible, too, makes decanting the frozen purées that much easier. As your baby gets older, it's a good idea to purchase some mini pots with lids, to freeze larger quantities of food.

A mini masher and bowl can be useful too, as it's ideal for mashing small quantities like one banana or a mix of potato, broccoli, and cheese, for example, and you can feed your baby from the same bowl.

Finally, look out for a mini thermos flask so that you can take warm, homemade purées with you when you are out and about.

Q I don't know how I'll have time to make purées every day. Do you have any advice?

A As a baby eats only tiny amounts, especially in the early stages of weaning, it saves time to make baby food in batches and freeze extra portions in ice-cube trays for future meals. If you cook for a few hours at the weekend you could make all your baby's food for a week.

Q What is the best way to cook my baby's vegetables?

A Steaming vegetables is a great way to preserve their fresh taste and nutrients. Vitamins B and C are water soluble and are destroyed by cooking, especially when boiled in water. Broccoli, for example, loses over 60 per cent of its antioxidants when boiled, but less than 7 per cent when steamed.

Microwaving is also a good way of cooking vegetables. It requires very little water and the soluble vitamins B and C aren't leached out into the water (as they are when boiled). It's a very quick way of cooking too – and is an ideal way to cook fish, which takes just a few minutes. Don't be put off by microwaving – it is a safe way to cook as long as you follow the manufacturer's instructions.

Q At what temperature should I serve my baby's food?

A Your baby's food should be given at body temperature (see page 32), as babies' palates are very sensitive. If re-heating food in a microwave, heat until piping hot, allow to cool, then stir thoroughly to get rid of any hot spots and check the temperature before giving it to your baby.

Q Are frozen purées as nutritious as fresh?

A If you freeze your purées as soon as they are cool, and cover them with a lid, they are as nutritious as fresh, and will remain so for about eight weeks in the freezer (see box on opposite page).

Leaving a purée sitting around in the fridge means that its nutritional content will be slowly compromised, and freezing it at this stage will certainly not make it more nutritious.

Freezing does effectively preserve nutrients, so if you know that you won't be using all of the purée you have just made, it's a good idea to freeze it as soon as it has cooled and use it when it's needed, at which point it will be perfectly fresh and nutritious. Label the food with the contents and expiry date.

Thaw foods by defrosting them in the fridge overnight, or by taking them out of the freezer several hours before a meal. Sometimes you may need to add a little liquid when reheating frozen food, as freezing can cause it to dry out.

PREPARATION TIME 2 MINUTES | COOKING TIME ABOUT 15 MINUTES | MAKES 4 BABY PORTIONS

carrot purée

Root vegetables make the **perfect first weaning food** because
of their naturally sweet taste and smooth texture when puréed.
Orange-coloured root vegetables are rich in beta-carotene, which
is essential for growth, healthy skin, **good vision, and strong bones**.
The recipe will also work for sweet potato, parsnip, or swede.

2 carrots, washed and peeled or
scraped, then chopped or sliced

1 Put the carrots in a steamer set over boiling water
and cook for 15–20 minutes until really tender
(the smaller the pieces, the quicker they'll cook).
Alternatively, place the carrots in a saucepan
and just cover with boiling water. Bring back
to the boil, then reduce the heat and simmer for
about 15 minutes or until tender; drain, reserving
the cooking liquid.

2 Purée the carrots until very smooth, adding some
of the cooking liquid or some of the water in the
bottom of the steamer. The amount of liquid you
add really depends on your baby – you may need
to add more if your baby finds it hard to swallow.

3 Allow to cool, then serve one portion and freeze
the remainder in ice cube trays or small pots. If
frozen, thaw overnight in the fridge, then reheat in
the microwave or a small pan until piping hot. Stir
and allow to cool before serving.

feeding basics

Every baby is different, both in the way they approach mealtimes and in their individual tastes. There is plenty to consider when you begin weaning, but **try to relax** as you introduce your little one to solid foods, and choose amongst these **tried-and-tested solutions** for the hurdles you might encounter.

Q Where is the best place to feed my baby?

A At first, you may want to feed your baby in her bouncer or even on your lap. As soon as she is able to sit up, it's a good idea to feed her in a highchair in the kitchen, at or by the kitchen table. She'll become used to the concept that people sit down for a meal (hopefully together, as well!), and at a table. Your little one will also understand that when she sits down in her highchair, it's meal time, and not playtime or anything else. She's more likely to concentrate on eating, if this is what she expects. It will also save you a great deal of hassle in the future if she always eats her meals in the same place, as she will understand that dinner in front of the television is not an option.

Finally, it goes without saying that kitchens are much easier than sitting rooms to clean up after your baby has created her usual mess!

Q How often does my baby need to eat solids during the first few weeks?

A Begin by offering solids once a day, around a normal "meal time". Midday is a good time to start, as most little ones won't be too tired, and therefore more willing to try new things. This will also give your baby time to digest the new food, and not struggle with wind during the night. Don't wait until your baby is starving, because he'll want only one thing – his usual milk! Over the next month or so, you can increase the number of solid food meals.

Q When should my baby be eating three meals a day?

A By the age of seven, eight, or nine months your baby should be eating three meals a day, and be ready to enjoy a wide variety of tastes. She should have doubled her birth weight, and a diet of milk may not be enough for her, so it's important to give her red meat, which is a good source of iron and zinc, and oily fish, such as salmon or tuna, which contain essential fatty acids that are important for your baby's brain development. Don't give your baby more than two portions of oily fish a week.

⭐ **did you know …**

that you can introduce age-appropriate cutlery to your baby from the outset? Choose soft plastic implements with no sharp edges or points, and which fit neatly in his little hand. Most babies do not develop the skills necessary to feed themselves using cutlery until much later – at the age of two or three, and sometimes even later. That isn't to say, however, that they cannot attempt to do so. It's a good idea to encourage him to try, as you feed him alongside.

Q When do babies feed themselves?

A This won't happen for a little while. At around the age of ten or eleven months, babies often refuse to be spoon fed and prefer to feed themselves. The more you encourage your baby to feed himself, the more proficient he will become – encourage him to pick up finger foods, and to have a small spoon or fork from his first days of weaning. He may use his hands to eat for many months to come, and this is to be encouraged as well, as babies learn to explore food in this way, and learn about textures and consistencies, and he'll be more likely to try things that he may reject when you offer it on a spoon.

Q My baby flings her plate across the room, and wipes her hands everywhere; how can I discourage her?

A A little mess is to be expected, and it's important to allow babies to investigate solid foods with their hands – it is a perfectly normal part of development, and helps them master the art of finger feeding, which leads to self-feeding. Throwing a plate is probably not intentional, but another experiment! You can also make life easier by investing in a bowl that sticks to her tray with a suction cup.

Q How much food does my baby need?

A Your baby needs only a little food at the outset – perhaps a tablespoon or two of purée. After you have introduced a number of different foods, you can start blending together purées, and offering fruits, vegetables, as well as meat and fish, and wholegrains or pulses, such as rice, and pasta, at the same meal. You are offering him variety and new tastes at first, which will build up to form the basis of a healthy meal. Your baby will also let you know whether what you are providing is enough.

Q Should I avoid feeding my baby too close to bedtime?

A In the early days it is a good idea to avoid feeding your baby too late, as some babies struggle to digest their foods at first. Give her her main "meal" at lunchtime, and then something gentle and nourishing in the evening, such as cheesy mashed potatoes with broccoli.

mostly milk

Weaning can sometimes be overwhelming for your baby, and **he'll take comfort** in his regular milk feeds. What's more, the nutrients in his milk will support his **growth and development** while he gets to grips with the whole new world of **tastes and textures**.

Q **My baby doesn't seem remotely interested in anything but milk – how can I encourage her?**

A At the outset of weaning, it is not crucial that your baby has other fluids, as her usual milk will offer her plenty to keep her hydrated. You can tempt her by offering her a new, brightly coloured cup and allowing her to help herself. You can also give her a cup of water with every meal, so that she becomes used to seeing it there, and considers it a normal part of her meal.

When she has reached eight or nine months and is drinking less milk, you can offer some water. If she won't drink water, you can offer some heavily diluted fruit juice (1 part juice to 10 parts water). Give this after the meal to avoid filling her up, and to help her body absorb the iron from her food. Try also offering her milk in a cup, and gradually diluting it with cooled, boiled water, until there is virtually no milk remaining.

Q **My eight-month-old shows no interest in food; will he be getting enough from breast milk?**

A While some babies are ready for solids by six months or even a little earlier, others take more time. If this is the case, it is important that you see a healthcare professional, as although breast milk is extremely nutritious, it does not contain quite enough iron or vitamin D for babies. It is important that your baby doesn't become deficient in these, and he may require a vitamin supplement.

Furthermore, there is evidence to suggest that babies who are "late" weaners may not take to solid food easily, and resist foods with strong tastes or unusual textures. It's also important to introduce solid food sooner rather than later to give a non-allergic baby a chance to become used to potentially allergenic foods (see page 46).

Make sure you seek advice from a healthcare professional, and continue to offer your baby solid food once or twice a day. If he isn't interested, don't make a fuss. You could try some finger foods (see page 61), which may be more appealing, and which can be "gummed" or sucked until he's ready to take his first bite.

Q I've stopped breastfeeding my six-month-old; will she need formula now?

A Yes, until they reach the age of 12 months, babies need formula milk or breast milk to ensure that they get all of the nutrients they need for optimum growth and development.

"Follow-on" milk, which is higher in iron, may be appropriate at this stage, especially if your baby is a very fussy eater. Discuss this with your doctor or health visitor first.

You can offer solid food, formula, and breast milk together, if that suits you. There is no reason to give up breastfeeding at six months unless both you and your baby are ready. Your baby will need several milk feeds a day until she is a year old.

It's also worth noting that you can use full fat cow's milk, as well as formula, in cooking for your baby or with her cereal at this age.

Q Do I need to use a bottle or can my seven-month-old drink from a cup?

A If your baby can master a cup, and drinks his milk and any other fluids, such as water or baby juice, happily, then there is no reason to introduce a bottle. Many breastfed babies go straight on to a cup from an early age, and manage to get everything they need this way. Your baby may miss the comfort of an evening or morning feed, as drinking from a cup doesn't require the same "sucking", nor a cuddle with mum or dad, so don't rush to lose the bottle or to give up breastfeeding unless you need to. While long-term bottle-feeding can potentially cause damage to teeth, and become a habit, it is also very much a part of babyhood, which is most certainly not over by nine months!

Q Is it safe to mix breast milk with purées?

A You can use breast milk in much the same way as ordinary milk or formula, and blend it into baby purées to add nutrition, and to make them more palatable and "familiar". It is important for babies to have quite runny purées at the outset, as they will "suck" rather than use their lips to remove food from the spoon, and it can take some time to get used to dealing with the food in their mouths before swallowing. Mixing her food with breast milk will ensure it is the right consistency. Remember that, like purées, breast milk has a "shelf life" of 48 hours, and should not be used after this time; add breast milk to purées as and when you use them.

offering other drinks

A little heavily diluted juice or water with meals will do no harm, and accustom your baby to drinking from a cup. In fact, a vitamin C-rich juice given at mealtimes will help aid absorption of iron from your baby's food. However, remember that your baby's tummy is very small, and it is easily filled up by drinks, when food is what is really required. Just 30–60ml (1–2 fl oz) of water or juice is fine with meals, preferably after he's eaten. He will likely get all the fluids he needs from milk and purées until weaning is complete.

Q **My baby was interested in her new "diet" for a short time, but now wants only breast milk again. What should I do?**

A It's not unusual for babies to regress during the weaning process. It's a big developmental leap to adjust to eating new and different foods, and to give up the comfort of milk feeds. Some babies may be slower to adjust to this change, and reluctant to carry on. Try to make the process easier, by offering her plenty of milk after her "meals". If she knows that she's still getting what she wants, and that her comfort feeds have not been replaced by a hard spoon with unfamiliar contents, she'll be less likely to object. Don't give up, though. She'll eventually become accustomed to the new routine, and look forward to mealtimes, particularly if they are pleasant, and she is praised.

⭐ **diluting juice**

It's best to offer water to your baby, but if she won't drink water, offer heavily diluted fruit juice (1 part juice to 10 parts water) after a meal. This is because juice is full of calories, which can fill your baby's tummy, without offering her the range of nutrients that she needs. Also, some juices can be quite acidic, and hard on your baby's tummy. Finally, juice is very high in natural fruit sugars, which can potentially cause tooth decay and encourage a sweet tooth.

Q **My baby has gone off breastfeeding completely since I introduced solids; is there any way to encourage him to continue?**

A It is very important that your baby continues to have breast milk or formula until he is a year old (see page 45). If he won't take to your breast, then you will have to consider introducing a bottle.

Why not try breastfeeding more during periods when your baby is looking for a cuddle and some comfort, rather than something to eat? Bedtime, and first thing in the morning, are ideal times to have a good, long feed, and your baby will probably get most of what he needs from these two feeds. You could also try offering your breast an hour or so before his meals, so that he gets the foremilk, and a little of the nutritious hind milk when he's hungry enough to want it. He can then eat a little later, and try different foods as you wean him.

Q **Can I use a little squash to get my baby to drink some water?**

A Even high-fruit squashes tend to contain high levels of sugar and/or artificial sweeteners, which are not recommended for young babies. Unless your baby has become accustomed to sweet drinks, such as full-strength fruit juices, she should not be resistant to drinking water, and introducing a sweetener will make the process of encouraging her to drink more water in future that much more difficult. Most babies in this age group will be getting the fluids they need from their normal milk feeds, and from their purées, and probably don't need to drink a lot more; however, if the only thing on offer is fresh water, this is what they will learn to drink, if and when they are thirsty.

understanding allergies

Food allergies are on the increase, but still remain uncommon in little ones, and are very often outgrown. **It helps to be aware** of the symptoms, and to know where to turn. The best advice is not to panic, and to **talk to your doctor** if you have any concerns.

Q How will I know if my baby has a food allergy?

A Food allergies are much more common among children in families with a history of allergy. Babies who suffer from eczema are particularly at risk – and the more severe the eczema, the more likely there is to be a food allergy. Some food allergies are fairly easy to spot – as soon as the food is eaten, often for the first or second time, a reaction occurs (see box, right).

Delayed allergies may also be a problem for infants. In the past, these were sometimes called food intolerance, but this isn't the correct term, because an intolerance doesn't involve the immune system. Delayed allergic reactions do involve the immune system, but parts of it that take longer to respond. This means it can be difficult to pinpoint a particular food as the problem, as sufferers may continue to eat and drink it. Milk, soya, egg, and wheat are often the main culprits, and symptoms include eczema, reflux, colic, poor growth, diarrhoea and constipation (see box, overleaf). These get better only when the food is removed from the diet. However, all of these symptoms commonly occur during childhood and an allergy is only one possible explanation. You'll need the help of an experienced doctor to diagnose a food allergy (see overleaf).

★ immediate food allergies

Moderate symptoms

These typically affect the skin, the respiratory system, and the gut. Seek medical advice.

- A flushed face, hives, or a red and itchy rash around the mouth, tongue, or eyes. This can spread across the entire body
- Mild swelling, particularly of the lips, eyes, and face
- A runny or blocked nose, sneezing, and watering eyes
- Nausea, vomiting, tummy cramps, and diarrhoea
- A scratchy or itchy mouth and throat

Severe symptoms (anaphylaxis)

This an emergency – call 999.

- Wheezing or difficulty in breathing
- Swelling of the tongue and throat, restricting the airways. This can cause noisy breathing (especially on breathing in), a cough or a change in your baby's cry or voice
- Lethargy, floppiness, or collapse

★ delayed food allergies

Symptoms include:

- Eczema
- Reflux (see page 36)
- Poor growth
- Swelling in the small bowel
- Constipation and/or diarrhoea
- Raising knees to chest with tummy pain
- Frequent distress and crying

Q We have a family history of allergies; should I avoid certain foods?

A If you have a history of allergy in your family (including asthma, hayfever, eczema, and food allergies), and your baby suffers from eczema, she is more likely to have food allergies.

It was thought that potentially allergenic foods (milk, eggs, tree nuts, shellfish, seafood, wheat, and soya) should be avoided until babies are a year old, and peanuts for the first three years of a child's life, but this advice has now been withdrawn. Recent studies suggest that there is no value in delaying the introduction of allergenic foods.

The jury is still out regarding what the best weaning policy is for babies at risk of food allergies, and more research is required. If your baby is in this "high-risk" category and you'd like more advice, it is a good idea to see your doctor or a dietitian.

Q How are allergies diagnosed?

A If you suspect an allergy, you must see a doctor with experience in allergy. There are many private allergy tests available, such as hair analysis and kinesiology, however these are costly, inaccurate, and can put your baby's health at risk.

The best way to diagnose immediate allergies, where the reaction occurs within two hours, is with a skin prick test and/or a blood test. These determine which foods, if any, are triggering allergic symptoms by detecting the presence of antibodies called IgE – which help to identify the problem foods. The allergens that will be tested are usually those about which you have expressed concern, although your doctor may also test other foods in the same group, other common foods (from the "big eight", for example: cow's milk, wheat, soya, fish, shellfish, eggs, peanuts, and tree nuts), or anything else that appears possible. The results must be interpreted by an experienced doctor.

Q What about delayed food allergies? Are these very difficult to diagnose?

A If your baby experiences a delayed reaction to a food (where symptoms take up to 48 hours to appear), the best way to diagnose the allergy is for you to keep a food and symptom diary, and eliminate the suspected food or foods for a minimum of two weeks, and see if the symptoms cease. The foods need to be reintroduced under the supervision of a doctor or dietitian who are experienced in allergy. It's never a good idea to try an elimination diet without support from an expert, as the nutrients lost in key parts of your baby's diet are crucial to his growth and development, and will need to be replaced.

new tastes and textures

With so many delicious, **nutritious foods available**, you can be forgiven for becoming confused about what your baby should and shouldn't be eating. It's a **good idea to start slowly**, and take your time in introducing new foods. Once your baby gets used to the idea that **food can be fun and delicious**, she'll be an instant convert.

Q **Should I put off introducing wheat until later?**

A Wheat can be introduced to your baby from six months onwards. If there is a history of allergies in your family (see page 58), you may wish to introduce new foods one at a time and over two or three consecutive days, so that if there is a reaction, you'll know what has caused it.

Q **When can I introduce dairy produce?**

A By six months, it is perfectly safe to add some cow's milk and dairy products (such as yogurt, cheese, and butter) to food. You can give cow's milk with your baby's cereal, or use it when making a cheese sauce, for example. Again, if there is a history of allergies in your family, follow the advice given above when introducing a new food.

Cow's milk, and other milks, such as soya, rice, and oat milk, can be used in the preparation of your baby's food, but should not be offered in place of his normal milk feeds, which need to be continued until he is at least 12 months old.

When cooking, always use full-fat, rather than low-fat milk, until your baby is at least two years old, as he'll need the calories to fuel his rapid growth.

Q **Is it OK to give my six-month-old baby yogurt?**

A It's fine to introduce yogurt to your baby from six months. Be careful when choosing yogurts, however, as many contain artificial sweeteners and flavourings that aren't appropriate for babies. Ideally, you'll want to find one without any added sugar, and blended with fresh fruit purée. Many babies prefer fromage frais, because of its creamier consistency; choose one that is free from artificial additives and sweeteners. Otherwise, you are better off adding a little of your own purée to some plain yogurt, and introducing dairy produce this way. Live yogurt is fine for little ones, and will encourage healthy digestion, but all milk products offered to babies should be pasteurized. Make sure you choose whole-milk yogurts, never low-fat, as your baby will need these extra calories.

Q Can I give my baby pasta?

A Once your baby is able to chew, stirring tiny cooked pasta shapes into her purées is a great way of introducing texture. As your baby gets used to the concept of chewing, the size of the pasta shapes can increase. This is a good way to gradually move from smooth purées to more challenging textures.

Larger pasta shapes, such as penne, farfalle, or fusilli, make good "finger food". Make sure the shapes are big enough for your baby to hold.

Q What other grains are healthy and suitable for babies?

A It is a very good idea to offer different grains, not only because they provide your baby with a variety of nutrients, but they also introduce him to different textures and tastes. Oats are a good starter food – try your baby with soaked porridge or the Creamy apple and oat purée recipe on page 65. Rice, couscous, and quinoa are good, too, as they are quite soft to chew. A little later on, you can introduce grains like millet and  buckwheat, but at first, choose grains that are easily digestible and won't fill up your baby's tummy before he's tasted the other foods on offer.

Q When should I introduce eggs?

A Eggs can be safely introduced at about six months of age. Make sure they are fully cooked, however, and not served runny or soft-boiled. Egg allergy is less common than people think, but children with a family history of allergy or those who suffer from eczema are more likely to have an allergy to eggs. If your baby is in this "high-risk" group, you may wish to introduce egg over two or three consecutive days, so that if there is a reaction, you'll know what has caused it.

Q At what age should I introduce fish?

A Fish can be introduced at six months. It's sometimes hard to find jars of purée containing fish, which is why making fish dishes for your baby is especially important. White fish, such as cod, haddock, sole, or plaice, are good first bets as they're mildly flavoured, and easily digestible. See the Sole, sweet potato and broccoli purée on page 63, which is a great recipe for introducing little ones to their first taste of fish. Oily fish, such as tuna and salmon, can be introduced at six months too, and these are rich in essential fatty acids, which are important for your baby's brain development. Mixed with root vegetables, such as carrot or sweet potato, these can make tasty purées for your baby.

It's important not to put little ones off eating fish, because it's such a great food. If overcooked, it can be dry and tasteless – it needs just a few minutes in a pan or mircrowave. Also, be vigilant in removing all of the bones.

As with all new foods, if there is a history of allergies in your family (see page 58), you may wish to introduce fish over a few consecutive days, so you can watch for a reaction.

Q Can I give my baby chicken?

A Yes, do introduce chicken and other meats, once she is comfortable with simple purées. Chicken, in particular, is a great first meat, as it has a mild flavour and is tender. The dark meat actually contains twice as much iron and zinc as the white meat, so try to give her the dark meat as well as the breast. For a tasty way to introduce chicken, see the Chicken and corn chowder recipe on pages 66–67. You can also make this with the chicken thigh meat – just cook the chicken a little longer. Some babies object to the texture of meat, and chicken can be a little stringy if it is overcooked without liquids. Slow poaching will usually produce light, tasty, and easily chewed chicken.

Q Are there any foods we should be avoiding?

A Unpasteurized juices and unpasteurized cheeses, such as brie, camembert, and goat's cheese, and blue cheeses, should be avoided in your baby's first year. Honey should also be off the menu until your baby reaches 12 months as it can cause infant botulism. Although this is very rare, it's best to be safe, as a baby's immune system is too immature to cope with the bug. Whole nuts should not be given to children before the age of five due to the risk of choking.

You may want to avoid fatty foods, processed meats, and anything containing artificial ingredients or sweeteners, as well as salt and sugar, for as long as you can.

Otherwise, feel free to experiment, and enjoy introducing your baby to the wonderful world of food. Persevere; if he doesn't like something, try it again at a later date.

Q Are there any finger foods appropriate for this age group?

A Finger foods are to be encouraged, because they help your baby to develop the skills necessary to feed herself, and to persuade her to chew and explore new tastes and textures at her own speed. First finger foods should be able to be "gummed" to a suitable consistency for swallowing (see the three stages of finger foods, below). Always supervise your baby due to the risk of choking.

⭐ finger foods

1. **Melt in the mouth:**
- Steamed soft carrot sticks, broccoli, and cauliflower florets
- Pear, banana, apple, blueberries, mango, peach, strawberries
- Avocado

2. **Bite and dissolve:**
- Steamed new potatoes
- Toast fingers
- Miniature rice cakes
- Well-cooked pasta shapes
- Mini sandwiches with soft fillings (see page 97)

3. **Bite and chew:**
- Oven-baked potato or sweet potato wedges
- Cucumber sticks
- Cheese, cut into sticks
- Small chunks of fish or chicken
- Dried apricots and apple rings

Q At what age can my baby tolerate "lumps"?

A Different babies tolerate lumps at different stages, but most babies will give foods with lumpier textures a go at around eight months, once you've established a good repertoire of purées and finger foods, although you may have to wait a little longer if your baby finds them difficult to manage.

To begin with, try mashing food, then add in lumpy foods with a soft texture, such as rice, couscous, or tiny pasta shapes, to your baby's favourite purée. Babies prefer overall lumpiness to a smooth purée with an occasional lump. At first your baby may refuse anything other than smooth purées, but over time, he'll learn to control food in his mouth, and then chew, "gum", and then swallow them.

If he gags or seems distressed, don't worry; simply go back to his regular purées for a week or so, and then try him again with smaller pieces of mashed foods.

Q My baby has six teeth; is she able to bite and chew now?

A The ability to chew is not just about having the teeth to do so! Some babies manage to eat a wide variety of foods with no teeth at all, mastering the art of "gumming" to make them smooth enough for swallowing. Biting is obviously more difficult without teeth, but it's amazing what babies can achieve when they set their minds to it!

It's absolutely worth introducing some finger foods that will require your baby to bite off pieces and chew or gnaw. Start to introduce lumpier textures as soon as she seems ready, then mash, rather than purée her meals, until she has enough teeth to chew whole, well-cut foods properly.

Q At what age can I chop foods finely instead of puréeing them?

A The advice same goes here, really. Keep an eye on your baby, and assess what he's able to manage. If he is comfortable with a variety of finger foods and lumpy purées, then move on to chopping and mashing, and leave your food processor for more difficult foods, such as dried fruits, seeds and nuts, and tougher cuts of meat.

★ did you know ...

that many babies who refuse lumpy foods will happily chew on finger foods? Introducing lumpier textures can be a stressful time for parents, but don't despair, because if your baby is chewing on finger foods, this means he can easily cope with lumpier textures. The muscles a baby uses to chew are the same ones used for speech, so encouraging your baby to chew will help his speech development too. See the finger food ideas on the previous page.

PREPARATION TIME 8 MINUTES | COOKING TIME 6–8 MINUTES | MAKES 3 BABY PORTIONS

sole, sweet potato, and broccoli purée

When **introducing fish** to babies, I like to start with something like sole or plaice as it is very tender and mild. Here I **combine it with sweet vegetables**, which should help to tempt the tastebuds. You can also substitute salmon for the white fish.

½ sweet potato (about 200g/7oz), peeled and cut in small dice

2 broccoli florets (about 40g/1½ oz in total), cut in small pieces

115g (4oz) sole, plaice, or other white fish fillet, skinned and cut into little-finger size strips

4 tbsp milk

20g (¾oz) Gruyère or Emmenthal cheese, grated

1 Spread the sweet potato and broccoli out in a steamer (or use a metal colander set over a pan of simmering water). Cover and steam for 6–8 minutes until really tender.

2 Meanwhile, put the fish into a small saucepan, cover with the milk, and cook for about 2 minutes or until it flakes easily. Remove from the heat and stir in the cheese until melted. Put the vegetables and fish mixture in a blender or baby mouli and purée. Add a little more milk, if necessary.

3 Cool as quickly as possible (put the purée in a glass bowl set in a second bowl of ice and stir for 4–5 minutes), then cover and put into the fridge. Or freeze in individual portions; thaw overnight in the fridge when needed.

4 To serve, heat the purée in a microwave or small saucepan until piping hot, stirring occasionally and adding a little more milk if necessary. Cool to warm and check the temperature before serving.

PREPARATION TIME 7 MINUTES | COOKING TIME 10–15 MINUTES | MAKES ABOUT 8 BABY PORTIONS

creamy apple and oat purée

"Eating" rather than "cooking" apples will make a sweet purée, with **plenty of nutrients** and healthy fibre. Oats make a great addition to your baby's diet; they are **packed with vitamins**, minerals, and essential fatty acids. Best of all, they help to stabilize your baby's blood sugar levels, **keeping him calm and full of energy**.

3 eating apples, such as Spartan or Pink Lady, peeled, cored, and thinly sliced

2 tbsp water

Pinch of ground cinnamon (optional)

1 tsp agave nectar (optional – to add more sweetness)

Per portion

1 tbsp baby oats

2 tbsp breast milk or formula

1 Put the apples in a saucepan with the water. Bring to the boil, then reduce the heat, cover, and cook very gently for 10–15 minutes until soft.

2 Add the cinnamon, if using, and purée in a blender, or mash. Sweeten with the agave nectar, if using. Cool the purée and keep in the fridge until needed, or freeze in individual portions and thaw as required.

3 To serve, warm one portion (approx 2 tbsp) of the apple purée and stir in the oats and milk. Cool slightly and check the temperature before serving.

PREPARATION TIME 10 MINUTES | COOKING TIME 10 MINUTES | MAKES 4–6 BABY PORTIONS

chicken and corn chowder

Chicken is a **good first meat for babies** as it is tender and has a mild flavour. Mixing it with sweetcorn in a smooth chowder is **a clever way to introduce chicken** to your baby. Another good combination is chicken with sweet potato and apple.

1 skinless, boneless chicken breast, cut into 2cm (¾in) cubes

200g (7oz) can naturally sweet sweetcorn in water, drained

5 tbsp water

1 potato, peeled and diced

1–2 tbsp breast milk or formula

1 Put the chicken, sweetcorn, and measured water in a small heatproof bowl and set the bowl in a large saucepan. Put the potato in the saucepan alongside the bowl. Pour boiling water over the potato in the pan so the water comes halfway up the sides of the bowl. Bring the water back to the boil, then reduce the heat, cover, and cook for about 10 minutes or until the potato and the chicken are cooked through.

2 Lift the bowl out of the pan. Drain the potatoes and put them in a baby mouli set over a bowl. Add the chicken, sweetcorn, and cooking liquid from the bowl and purée the mixture (puréeing with a mouli will get rid of the skins from the sweetcorn; if you use a blender, you will have to pass the mixture through a sieve after puréeing). Add a little milk, if necessary, to make a soft, smooth consistency. Cool quickly, then chill. Or, freeze in individual portions; thaw overnight in the fridge when needed.

3 To serve, heat in a saucepan or microwave until piping hot. Allow to cool slightly and check the temperature before serving.

food from a jar

All of us are busy, and it does make sense to rely on **some ready-made purées** for your baby from time to time. Balanced by a regular selection of healthy, home-cooked fare, **your baby will thrive** and learn to appreciate different tastes and consistencies.

Q Is there anything wrong with using jars occasionally?

A There is nothing wrong with relying on the odd jar of food, to get you through a busy period, or when you are travelling and do not have the means to keep fresh purées cool. The problem is that their nutritional content may be compromised because of the heat treatment necessary to make them safe to eat throughout a fairly long shelf life.

These foods tend to be bland, and lack the natural flavour and aroma of fresh foods, which can mean, in the long-term, that your baby's palate is shifted in favour of less challenging flavours and textures. Giving fresh food from the beginning tends to make the transition to family food easier.

It's worth noting that if you think you don't have time to prepare homemade baby food, it doesn't have to be as time-consuming as you may have thought. See the box, right, for quick tips.

Q My baby will only eat food from a jar; what can I do?

A Not surprisingly, many babies are reluctant to move back or on to homemade foods once they have been introduced to the bland, unchallenging flavours and textures of jars.

First of all, you can simply refuse to buy any more jars. Your baby is young enough to be able to shake a bad habit fairly quickly, and if she realizes that there is nothing else on offer, she'll undoubtedly eat it, after kicking up a bit of a fuss.

If she's stubborn, you can consider mixing some of her favourite jarred food with your own purées, gradually adding more of your homemade concoctions until she is accustomed to the taste and the texture. Experiment with different flavours, and try to come up with combinations that appeal to her. If she's very fond of her shop-bought apple purée, for example, mix a little of that into some steamed, puréed carrots. You can also start introducing your baby to your family meals, by offering her a little on the side in the form of a finger food. She'll be more likely to experiment with something that she can pick up and try herself, and which looks much like what her siblings or parents are eating.

Q What additives and preservatives should I avoid when I need to use jars?

A Most manufacturers are fairly responsible when it comes to preparing baby foods, and the most damaging food additives do not usually appear. However, this is not always the case, and if your baby is venturing off the beaten track to try different foods, there are quite a few things that it's advisable to look out for.

The first are sugar and salt, which are not appropriate for babies, and should be avoided for as long as possible. There is also some new, convincing evidence that sodium benzoate, tartrazine, sunset yellow, and some red food colourings can cause problems, particularly in children who may show some signs of attention deficit and hyperactivity disorder (ADHD). Obviously you won't have a clue whether or not your baby falls into this category, but you may wish to avoid these additives anyway. They offer no nutritional goodness whatsoever, and may cause harm. It's also important to avoid nitrates, although occasional use is OK.

Finally, avoid artificial sweeteners as much as possible. These are comprised of chemicals that may have a detrimental effect on health.

Fresh and natural is your best bet, so avoid anything with a name that resembles something from a chemistry textbook.

Q Should I avoid GM foods?

A GM (genetically modified) foods should probably be off the menu. Although we are still not sure what the long-term effects on health might be, these foods are very much an unknown quantity, and until further research is completed, I'd recommend that you avoid them.

Q Do I need to choose organic fruits and vegetables for my baby?

A There is no conclusive evidence that organic foods are healthier than those that are conventionally farmed; however, some studies suggest that organic produce has higher levels of key vitamins and minerals. Also, the long-term effects of the pesticides routinely used on non-organic crops is still unknown, so some people suggest avoiding pesticides until more is known about these chemicals. The bottom line is that there is still a lot of conflicting advice and evidence, so it's up to you. Many of us find that some organic foods are expensive, so if you can't afford them, don't feel bad. Your baby will be perfectly fine on a diet of ordinary fruit and vegetables.

★ no time to cook?

Lots of fruits such as banana, papaya, and peaches, do not require cooking provided they are ripe – simply mash them with a fork to make instant baby food. These are also great when you have no equipment to make purées on holiday (see pages 74–75 for recipes). Also, If you get into the habit of cooking for an hour or so once or twice a week for your baby, and freezing your efforts, you'll soon build up a good selection of homemade "jars" to choose from.

balance and variety

As parents **we have a responsibility** to ensure that our little ones get everything they need to grow up **strong and healthy**. That doesn't mean serving boring "health" food, but encouraging a **fresh, delicious and varied diet** that will provide your baby with all the key nutrients she needs.

Q My baby will eat only fruit purées; does this matter?

A In the short-term, it is not a big problem, as your baby will be getting plenty of nutrients from fruit. However, it won't give your baby protein or iron. It does also become an issue if your baby develops a sweet tooth, as he will be reluctant to try anything that is not "sugary", which can make introducing other foods that much more difficult. Fruit is very healthy, but it can cause a surge in blood sugar, followed by a crash, which can leave your baby tired and irritable. Moreover, it can, over time, cause tooth decay.

It's much better to have a mix of both fruit and vegetables. Try different combinations, such as spinach and kiwi, parsnip and apple, or mango with carrots. Try, too, introducing sweeter vegetables, such as sweetcorn, peas, sweet potato, and squash on their own. Their natural sweetness can match the sweetness of fruits.

Q When do I have to start making sure my baby's diet is balanced?

A When you begin weaning, you are offering tastes of a variety of different foods to accustom your baby to the process of eating rather than just drinking her usual milk, and also to encourage her to develop a taste for different flavours and textures. At the outset, she'll probably have only one or two small meals a day, heavily subsidized by her usual milk, which provides the vast majority of the nutrients she requires. When her milk feeds become less frequent, and she is eating more at mealtimes, usually around eight or nine months, it becomes increasingly important that she gets a variety of different nutrients from each of the main food groups: carbohydrates, fats, protein, and vitamins and minerals.

It's not as hard as you may think to ensure that she has a balanced diet. If you aim for plenty of fresh fruit and vegetables, with different foods presented every day or so, plus some good-quality protein, such as red meat, poultry, pulses, and fish, some healthy carbs (wholegrains are your best choice here), and some dairy produce and eggs, too, your baby will be getting exactly what she needs.

Q We want to raise our baby as a vegetarian; is there anything extra he needs at this age?

A To begin with, a vegetarian baby's diet is the same as for other babies – a variety of fresh fruits and vegetables. Introduce your baby to the huge variety of delicious vegetables available, and encourage him to try as many as he can, so that your options are not limited as he gets older.

The iron a baby inherits from his mother runs out at around six months, so from six or seven months, you should include iron-rich foods, such as pulses (lentils and chickpeas), leafy green vegetables, eggs, and dried aprocots, in your baby's diet. Wholegrain cereals are also a good source, but do not give your baby too many, as his tummy is only small. It's important to include foods like cheese and well-cooked eggs too. These are good sources of protein and vitamin B12, which your baby needs for growth and development.

Being vegan, however, does mean cutting out two further main food groups: dairy and egg. These must be carefully replaced, so it may be useful to see a trained dietitian. Also, if you give your baby at least 600ml (20fl oz) of fortified infant soya formula daily, until he is two, he shouldn't need supplements.

Q How can I introduce pulses into my baby's diet?

A Lentils, peas, chickpeas, and beans, such as butter beans and cannellini beans, are all good first foods, and will offer plenty of protein and iron, as well as fibre and B vitamins, so are great for vegetarian babies. Cook them thoroughly, and purée them with vegetables to make them more tasty, and easier to swallow and digest (see my red lentils purée recipe on page 107).

Your baby doesn't need many of any type of pulse at this stage and age – a serving would constitute no more than four or five individual peas or beans, or a spoonful of lentils. So even adding a teaspoon of cooked pulses to your baby's normal purée, and whizzing them together, will provide some added nutrition, and a different, unique texture. Many babies love hummus – look out for brands with no added salt or make your own. Serve on toast fingers, pitta bread, or with carrot, cucumber, and other veggies.

★ did you know ...

that carrots and other brightly coloured fruits and vegetables contain highly nutritious nutrients known as carotenoids, which your baby's body converts to vitamin A? This vitamin is crucial for health and development, and encourages healthy vision, immune system function, and strong, healthy bones. If possible, steam rather than boil carrots, as this allows the beta-carotene to be more bio-available and readily used by the body.

feeding problems

Some babies find **the transition to solid foods** easy, while others can be more resistant. Try to stick to a daily routine, even if you are out and about, or on holiday. It's not always easy, but **with a little ingenuity** and a good thermos flask, you'll soon overcome any problems.

Q My baby refuses the same foods over and over again; how can I tempt him to eat more foods?

A Perseverance is the order of the day. Simply continue to offer the "new" foods over and over again, until they become familiar to your baby (see opposite page). You can try them in different combinations – for example, mixing spinach with some apple purée or even a little Parmesan cheese and his normal baby milk, adding apricots to sweet potato, and pear to peas. Once you find one or two things you know he likes, you can use these as a base for creating different blends.

Remember too that many babies have quite sophisticated tastes. Baby food doesn't have to be bland, and your little one may enjoy trying exciting tastes that you may not have considered, such as garlic or a touch of mild curry paste in the cooking.

Q Can you recommend some combinations of vegetables to appeal to my faddy baby?

A Some of the best vegetables are those that are sweet. Fortunately, most of these all contain good levels of vitamins and minerals, and, in particular, antioxidants, which will ensure that your child grows and develops, and maintains good health. See page 163 for more information.

Try sweet potato, squash, sweetcorn, peas, edamame beans, butter beans, carrots, potato, courgettes, parsnips, and even avocado. Any combination of these will work. See page 76 for my delicious Sweet potato and squash purée recipe. If your little one has already expressed a preference for fruit purées, you can blend a little into your vegetable blends for added sweetness and flavour. Don't be afraid to experiment. I like root vegetables together, such as parsnip, carrot and potato, or butternut squash with very ripe pear. Sweet vegetables, such as carrot, puréed with fish or chicken is also a favourite with many babies.

Again, persevere, if you can tempt your baby to eat vegetables early on, she'll be much more likely to continue.

Q My baby likes only one type of food, and refuses everything else; any advice?

A Babies easily become accustomed to the familiar, and if he's found a particular food he likes, such as apple purée or carrot purée, and had it offered on a number of occasions, he may be reluctant to try anything else – and he may also hold out until he gets what he wants. Don't underestimate the determination of even very young babies.

The best thing to do is to continue offering new foods; over time (and this can take up to 15 or 20 attempts in some cases), the new food will become familiar, and he'll accept it. Try mixing his favourite food with other fruits and vegetables, adding small quantities at the outset, and then gradually more until he is getting a variety of different tastes.

If your baby is very young, he may find the process of weaning a little upsetting – in fact, some babies are more sensitive to change than others – so it may help to mix new foods such as green vegetables with popular "first tastes", for example sweet-tasting root vegetables, to make them more comforting. Remember to take weaning slowly, and follow your baby's own pace. Some little ones take to it quickly and move on to a variety of different foods with no fuss; others need a little more time to adjust to the change.

It can also help to eat the same meals as your little one. If he sees you, and perhaps the rest of the family, clearly enjoying a variety of different foods, he may want to follow suit. Make a "mmmm" sound when you offer them; it may sound simple, but if he is convinced that what he is trying is delicious, he'll respond much more positively. Whatever you do, don't panic or make a fuss. Simply remove the food and try again later.

Q Is there any way to bring homemade purées on holiday?

A If you don't have far to travel, you can pack several trays of frozen purée along with some cool packs and other frozen items, to ensure they remain at the lowest possible temperature while in transit. This may not be feasible, though, and perhaps more trouble than it's worth.

There are, however, plenty of ways to make fresh purées that don't even require cooking, and if you have a kitchen to hand, you can easily whip up the odd fresh purée as and when you need to! Exotic fruits like mango, peach, or papaya make perfect baby food and they don't even need any cooking (see pages 102). See the following pages, too, for some great recipe suggestions, requiring little more than a knife, fork, and bowl. For older babies, a wedge of peeled mango or melon makes good finger food.

★ transporting purées

For days out, you could invest in a small wide-necked thermos flask that will keep your baby's purée warm. The cover will serve as your baby's food bowl. If there is a fridge at your destination, a good cool bag with an ice pack should keep your baby's purée fresh until you reach your destination. The purées will then last a couple of days in the fridge.

PREPARATION TIME 3–5 MINUTES | EACH RECIPE MAKES 1 BABY PORTION

quick fruit purées

It can be difficult to provide healthy, homemade food for your baby on holiday. These **simple, no-cook purées** can be prepared in just a few minutes with basic cutlery and your baby's feeding bowl.

avocado and banana or pear
★ Scoop out the flesh from ¼–½ small, ripe avocado and mash with a fork. Mash ¼–½ small, ripe banana or pear (peeled and cored). Beat into the avocado until smooth.

banana and mango
★ Peel ¼–½ small, ripe mango, remove the flesh, and mash with a fork. Mash ¼–½ small, ripe banana into the mango and beat well until smooth.

banana and peach
★ Pull the skin off 1 small, ripe peach with the help of a knife. Remove the stone and mash the flesh. Mash ¼–½ small, ripe banana into the peach and beat well until smooth.

cantaloupe melon
★ Scoop out the seeds from 1 small slice of ripe melon, then cut off the skin. Cut the flesh into small pieces. Mash with a fork, then beat until smooth.

pear (or pear with peach)
★ Peel and core 1 small, ripe pear (or ½ small pear and ½ small, ripe peach). Cut the flesh into small pieces and mash with a fork, then beat until smooth.

PREPARATION TIME 15 MINUTES | COOKING TIME 40 MINUTES | MAKES 5–6 BABY PORTIONS

sweet potato and squash purée

Babies' taste buds tend to be **tuned into sweet flavours,** so naturally sweet fruits and vegetables are popular early foods. **Orange fruits and vegetables** like butternut squash and sweet potato are naturally sweet and they are also high in beta-carotene, which is the **plant form of vitamin A.**

1 small or ½ large butternut squash, peeled, deseeded, and cut into 2.5cm (1in) cubes

1 sweet potato, peeled and cut into 2.5cm (1in) cubes

1 tbsp olive oil

2 tbsp water

A little breast milk or formula

1 Preheat the oven to 200°C (180°C fan), gas 6.

2 Lay a large piece of foil on a baking sheet and spread out the squash and sweet potato on the foil. Drizzle over the olive oil and water. Cover with a second large piece of foil and scrunch the edges of the two foil pieces together to form a parcel. Bake for about 30 minutes or until the vegetables are tender.

3 Cool the vegetables slightly, then transfer to a blender (including any liquid). Blend to a smooth purée. Thin the purée with breast milk or formula to the desired consistency. (If you are going to freeze the purée, add the milk after thawing.)

4 Freeze in individual portions. When needed, thaw for 1–2 hours at room temperature, then microwave or reheat in a small pan until piping hot. Stir and allow to cool before serving.

part of the family

While many of the **foods you offer your family** may be a little heavy-going for your young baby, there is no reason why you can't **involve him in family meals**, and purée some of the elements of every meal you prepare. Babies love to feel part of the crowd, and will enjoy **eating the same food as everyone else.**

Q My baby keeps reaching for food from my own plate; should I let her try?

A There is no reason that your baby shouldn't try the food on your plate, provided there is nothing there that could cause her to choke, or which may be inappropriate for babies (see page 61). In fact, eating from mum and dad's plate is a good way to introduce your baby to new flavours and tastes, and encourage her to join in with family meals from an early stage. If she particularly likes something, mash it up for her or give her a finger-food sized slice that she can manage herself.

Q We sometimes get takeaways, and my baby is keen for a taste; is this safe?

A As long as it's not too fatty or rich, or contains foods that are inappropriate for little ones (see page 61), you can most certainly offer small tastes. There is plenty of research to indicate that children's tastes are established in early childhood, and the more he learns to eat at an early age, the more varied his palate will be later on. If your baby has food allergies, you have to be particularly careful, as takeaways are often a source of hidden allergens.

Q Can I purée family food for my baby?

A By all means. There are some foods that are inappropriate for babies (see pages 61 and 69) and you should offer only healthy foods to your little one – avoid salt and sugar.

In the early stages, you will need to ensure that you make a purée that is liquid enough for your baby to slurp up from a spoon, as she won't have developed her chewing skills yet. It's also a good idea to establish a few first foods on their own – several types of fruit, and several types of vegetables, for example, before moving on to fish, chicken, and meat. If you launch straight into family meals, it can be difficult to work out which foods are problematic, in the event that there is a reaction (see pages 57–58).

Remember that first foods are just tastes, too, and your little one won't require a whole balanced meal for some months to come.

★ eating out

Babies can be adventurous eaters, and will probably be happy to pick at lots of things on your plate. If in doubt, give him plain pasta with a little cheese, bread, vegetables, mashed potato, well-cooked scrambled egg, risotto, and any fresh, ripe fruits, mashed until smooth. If there are no concerns about food allergies, and the food isn't too spicy or salty, feel free to offer your baby tastes of sauces too.

Q Should I offer snacks to my baby if she seems hungry between feeds?

A Snacks are not really essential at this age, as your baby will be getting most of her calories and nutrition from milk. If she is hungry between feeds, you could try offering another small meal, with some purée and finger foods. You should also be sure that she is getting enough milk between "meals" to keep her going. Once again, first foods are about "tastes", and not designed to fill your baby. If you are out and about, snacks can keep her going, but make sure they are healthy.

Soft ripe fruit such as nectarine or slices or chunks of banana and melon are a good start. Some little ones can manage toast fingers, pieces of bread, rice cakes, and even oatcakes (see the finger food ideas on page 61). Be sure to keep an eye on her in case she chokes.

Q My baby refuses to eat meat; how can I tempt him?

A It's not surprising that many little ones are not keen on meat. It can be very dry if it's not cooked properly, and difficult to chew if it has not been puréed properly. I would recommend cooking meat or chicken with root vegetables, such as chicken with sweet potato and apple, or beef with carrots and dried apricots. See the delicious recipe on the opposite page too. You can also try offering little batons of chicken for him to gnaw on, as he may enjoy helping himself rather than being spoon-fed, and he'll become accustomed to the taste and texture in this way.

Q At what age is it appropriate to serve dessert to my baby?

A Dessert is something that most children (and adults!) look forward to, in order to round off a meal. It is not necessary, but it does provide some incentive for finishing the main course! There is no reason why your little one can't have a healthy dessert, such as fresh fruit purée (see page 80 for Peach, apple, and pear purée), a healthy homemade biscuit or muffin, some dried fruit, or a yogurt or fresh fruit lolly at the end of a meal.

While every single expert insists that you should never offer a reward for eating a meal, there is no doubt that the prospect of something a little special will tempt children to have one taste or one more bite of their main meal. The secret is to create desserts that are as healthy as their main courses, but with enough sweetness or flavour to make them special. A baked apple with a little maple syrup and raisins would provide a treat for the whole family and can be puréed or mashed for your baby.

PREPARATION TIME 10 MINUTES | COOKING TIME 14–15 MINUTES | MAKES 2–3 BABY PORTIONS

beef, squash, and tomato purée

The **sweet squash** and tomatoes here help to make the flavour of beef more **palatable for fussy babies.** As your baby gets older, the cooked beef can be **mashed into the squash** and tomatoes, and served with small pasta shapes.

2 plum tomatoes

1 tsp olive oil

115g (4oz) extra-lean minced beef

¼ small butternut squash, peeled, deseeded, and grated

150ml (5fl oz) vegetable stock, or water

1 Cut a small cross in the top of each tomato. Put them in a heatproof bowl and cover with freshly boiled water. Leave to stand for 30 seconds, then drain and plunge in cold water. Peel off the skins. Cut the skinned tomatoes into quarters, scoop out the seeds, and chop the flesh.

2 Heat the olive oil in a large frying pan or wok and sauté the beef for 2–3 minutes, stirring well, until browned and crumbly. Add the squash and chopped tomato, and sauté, stirring, for a further 2 minutes or until the vegetables are softened. Add the stock and bring to the boil, then reduce the heat, cover, and simmer for about 10 minutes.

3 Cool slightly before puréeing the contents of the pan in a blender, adding a little extra boiled water if the purée is too thick.

4 Freeze in individual portions. When needed, thaw overnight in the fridge, then reheat until piping hot. Stir and allow to cool slightly before serving.

PREPARATION TIME 10 MINUTES | COOKING TIME 10 MINUTES | MAKES 4–6 BABY PORTIONS

peach, apple, and pear purée

Ripe, seasonal fruits can make a plain apple purée a little more interesting. I like to use peaches or nectarines, **but apricots or plums are also good**. If the fruit is not very sweet, you can add a teaspoon of agave nectar, which is available from health food shops and some supermarkets.

2 ripe peaches

1 eating apple, such as Spartan or Pink Lady, peeled, cored, and diced

1 ripe pear, peeled, cored, and diced

2 tbsp water

1 Cut a small cross in the top and bottom of each peach and put them in a heatproof bowl. Cover with freshly boiled water and leave to stand for 30 seconds, then drain and plunge in cold water. Peel off the skins. Cut the peaches into quarters, remove the stones, and dice the flesh.

2 Put the diced peaches, apple, and pear in a saucepan with the water. Bring to the boil, then cover, reduce the heat to low, and cook gently for about 10 minutes or until the juices have run from the peaches and the fruits are all soft.

3 Cool slightly, then tip into a blender and purée until smooth. Serve warm, or cool quickly and chill in the fridge before serving. The purée can be frozen in individual portions; thaw for 1–2 hours at room temperature when needed.

sophisticated tastes

There is no reason why your baby's food has to be bland! **Herbs, spices, and even a little wine** will help her to become accustomed to more sophisticated tastes. **The younger she is** when you start, the easier it will be for her to make the **transition to family food**.

Q **Can I add salt or pepper to my baby's purées to give them more flavour?**

A Pepper is fine, and can add some much needed spice to blander foods. Go easy, though – a little goes a long way with small babies. Try a few grains to see if he enjoys the taste, and then go from there. Make sure it's finely ground, however, as coming across a grain of coarsely chopped black pepper can be eye-watering, and put him off his meal!

Don't be tempted to add salt or sugar to your baby's food, however bland. Salt may harm your baby's kidneys and sugar will encourage a sweet tooth. A baby is not used to these tastes so will not miss them. If you do want to jazz up his purées, there are plenty of herbs that will do the job (see box, opposite), or consider adding flavours like garlic or mild curry powder to vegetable or meat dishes, and cinnamon or vanilla to fruit purées.

Q **At what age can my child have sugar?**

A Most foods contain natural sugars, and provide your child with a good source of energy. Cane sugar, which is refined, and has had all of its nutrients stripped from it, offers little more than calories, and can play havoc with your little one's blood sugar levels, leaving her tired, irritable, and tearful. Unless sugar is required for a particular recipe – in homemade cakes, pancakes, or muffins, for example, or to sweeten very tart fruit – I would recommend leaving it off the menu. It's much better to choose maple syrup, stevia, or molasses, which offer vitamins and minerals as well as sweetening, or to choose fruit juices or purées to sweeten, instead of sugar.

In reality, babies don't need additional sugar. They soon become used to the natural sweetness of fresh, wholesome foods, and develop a taste for them. We may think their foods are bland, but if that's what they are used to, and all they know, they'll be perfectly happy. I would recommend avoiding sugar for as long as you can – except, of course, on special occasions, when you may want to offer an ice-cream or some cake alongside the rest of the family.

Q Fruit and vegetable purées don't seem very substantial; can I add a little milk or cheese to fill him up?

A You can certainly add a little of his regular milk (formula or breast milk) or a little grated cheese for extra flavour and added nutrients – see page 84 for the delicious Cauliflower, potato, and cheese purée recipe. Remember, though, that first foods are not meant to be full meals, but rather small tastes to introduce little ones to various different foods. Your baby doesn't need to be full after his meals, as he will likely go on to have his normal milk feed soon after.

Q Are sugarless fruit spreads OK for young babies?

A Sugarless fruit spreads are fine for babies, as long as they do not contain artificial sweeteners. They are, however, very concentrated and, for that reason, very sweet, so only a little will be required. You may want to spread them on toast fingers, or to fill tiny sandwiches. They can also be used to sweeten plain wholewheat or oatmeal porridges, as well as used in cooking and baking, and will provide some extra vitamins and minerals.

Q My baby refuses formula milk; can I flavour it to make it more palatable?

A Formula is designed to be a balanced form of nutrition, and should not, ideally, have anything added to it. Your baby is too young to give up her regular milk, and you will need to persevere to encourage her to take formula regularly throughout the day. You can try incorporating formula milk into the meals you prepare, but it's unlikely she'll get enough to sustain her growth and development.

You may want to try switching formulas, to see if another brand has a taste that she finds more acceptable.

If all else fails, you could consider stirring in a little fruit juice or purée, but only if your baby is on solids. You must also ensure that you continue to mix up the formula according to the manufacturer's instructions. If your baby continues to refuse the formula, you may need a referral to a dietitian to provide you with individualized advice.

★ did you know ...

that herbs are a delicious and nutritious addition to your baby's food? They can spice up, or make more fragrant, foods that might otherwise seem a little flavourless. Any of the green herbs, such as coriander, basil, chives, and parsley can be added easily, and you can use rosemary and bay leaves while cooking fish, chicken, or vegetables. The more flavours to which your little one becomes accustomed while he's small, the wider the variety of likes that will be established.

PREPARATION TIME 10 MINUTES | COOKING TIME 13–15 MINUTES | MAKES 6 BABY PORTIONS

cauliflower, potato, and cheese purée

This purée is **very filling and thick,** so ideal for hungry babies. If you are using sweet potato **instead of regular white potato,** you can reduce the cooking time of the potato on its own to 3 minutes before you **add the cauliflower.**

1 potato or small sweet potato (175g/6oz), peeled and cut into 1cm (½in) cubes

¼ small cauliflower, cut in little florets

100g (3½oz) Red Leicester or Cheddar cheese, grated

2–4 tbsp breast milk or formula

1 Put the potato cubes in a steamer, spreading them out in one layer. Cover and steam for 5 minutes. Add the cauliflower to the steamer, spreading the florets evenly. Cover again and steam for a further 8–10 minutes until the vegetables are soft.

2 Transfer the vegetables to a blender and add the cheese and 2 tbsp of the breast milk or formula. Blend to a smooth purée, adding extra milk or formula if the purée is too thick.

3 Freeze in individual portions. When needed, thaw overnight in the fridge, then reheat until piping hot. Stir and allow to cool slightly, and check the temperature before serving.

food and health

Starting your little one on a diet of healthy, fresh food will encourage him to **eat well in the future**, and also improve his resistance to illness. Your baby may be **reluctant to eat when he is feeling** under the weather, but keeping him hydrated and offering small, nutrient-dense meals can help him to **recover quickly and easily**.

Q My baby has lost her appetite and seems to be losing weight; how can I tempt her to eat?

A It's always worrying when babies stop eating for whatever reason, and the first thing you need to do is to ascertain the cause. If she is unwell, she may be off her food for a short period of time, and begin eating again in a few days' time, and with a vengeance! Keeping her hydrated during this time, with plenty of fluids, is the most important thing. If she's teething she may find eating less comfortable. In this case, offer her cool purées or a fromage frais that will help to soothe her gums and a teething ring or cold flannel to "teethe" on.

Make sure that your baby is getting enough milk (see page 45). Once little ones start on solid food it's easy to think that they are eating "meals" and don't need their normal milk intake, but this is not the case, as it provides them with the calories they need, as well as their main nutrients.

You can try tempting her with different foods – Greek yogurt mixed with fruit purée, cheesy pasta that has been puréed until smooth, or vegetables with grated cheese. Persevere, you'll soon find something that she loves, and even if you have to offer it daily to encourage her, it's worth the effort.

Q Should I be worried if my baby is underweight for her height?

A If your baby has always been underweight, and is growing in length and developing normally, you have no need for concern. Many babies have smaller frames, and are more slightly built than the "average" baby, and he may well be the perfect weight for his frame, even if he comes out as being light in relation to his height.

A healthy baby will have plenty of energy, will be alert, growing normally (along roughly the same centile line on his baby growth chart; see page 34) and sleep and feed well. If you don't think he's growing or developing at the rate you would expect, follow your instincts and talk to your doctor. There may be something else at the root, which can be addressed. It's always important to see your doctor if your baby's feeding habits change dramatically, he loses weight, seems tired, or doesn't sleep well.

⭐ giving vitamins

For most babies vitamin supplements are probably unnecessary, so long as they are eating fresh food in sufficient quantity and drinking formula milk until the age of one. However the Department of Health recommends that if your baby is being breastfed (breast milk doesn't contain enough vitamin D) or is drinking less than 500ml (18fl oz) of infant formula a day, you should give him vitamin supplements from six months to two years of age. It's a good idea to ask your health visitor or doctor for advice.

Q Are there any foods that will help my baby to sleep?

A Your baby's main food, her regular milk, whether it is breast milk or formula, is ideal for setting her to sleep. Like all dairy produce, milk contains an amino acid called tryptophan, which encourages sleep (see page 165). Warm milk and a full tummy are a great way to lull a baby off to sleep. Proteins such as meat, fish, chicken, and lentils are the best source of tryptophan, however, so include these in her dinner to make her sleepy. An oaty porridge is a good choice too, as oats are naturally calming and relaxing. Carbohydrates a few hours before bed, such as rice or potatoes, can also make her sleepy and ready for bed.

Q My baby has diarrhoea; what should he eat?

A The most important thing to consider when your baby has diarrhoea is fluid. He will need plenty to replace what he has lost in loose bowel movements, and he will need even more to encourage the healing process. So begin by offering him regular milk, whether it is formula or, even better, breast milk, little and often, and giving small sips of water or rehydration fluid in between. Keep an eye out for signs of dehydration (see page 37).

If he's eating regular meals, these should be pared down to the essentials. Apple purée is particularly good and very ripe bananas can help to restore your baby's good bacteria, which can be wiped out in the case of a tummy bug. They're also easily digestible, and will provide your baby with energy. Plain baby rice and toast fingers are also good bets for your little one.

Q What are superfoods, and should I be including them now?

A It is a great idea to include as many superfoods as you can, as early as possible, as their health benefits are undeniable. They give babies the best tools to grow and develop.

Superfoods are foods that contain fantastic levels of key vitamins, minerals, and antioxidants (see page 163 for more information), which will enhance your baby's health and development on all levels. Popular superfoods for little ones include mango, sweet potato, papaya, berries, butternut squash, sweet pepper, leafy green vegetables, and carrots.

PREPARATION TIME 10 MINUTES | COOKING TIME 9–11 MINUTES | MAKES 5 BABY PORTIONS

superfoods purée

Superfoods have been identified as **those rich in vitamins, minerals, and antioxidants**. This purée contains turkey, spinach, and sweet potatoes, which all make the grade. You can also use **minced chicken thigh** instead of the turkey.

1 sweet potato, peeled and cut into 1cm (½in) cubes

2 tsp olive oil

1 small shallot, or small piece of onion, finely chopped

115g (4oz) minced turkey

2 handfuls of baby spinach leaves, washed but not dried

1 Put the sweet potato in a steamer and steam for about 6 minutes or until tender. Remove from the steamer and reserve the steaming water.

2 While the sweet potato is cooking, heat the oil in a large frying pan or wok, add the chopped shallot and turkey, and stir-fry for 2–3 minutes until the turkey is browned and crumbly. Add the spinach and sauté for 2–3 minutes until wilted.

3 Add the cooked sweet potato and 4 tbsp of the steaming water. Cover and simmer gently for 5 minutes.

4 Put the contents of the pan in a blender and blend to a purée. Thin with a little of the steaming water, if necessary. Cool quickly, then chill. Freeze in individual portions, then thaw overnight in the fridge when needed.

5 To serve, heat in a saucepan or microwave until piping hot. Allow to cool slightly and check the temperature before serving.

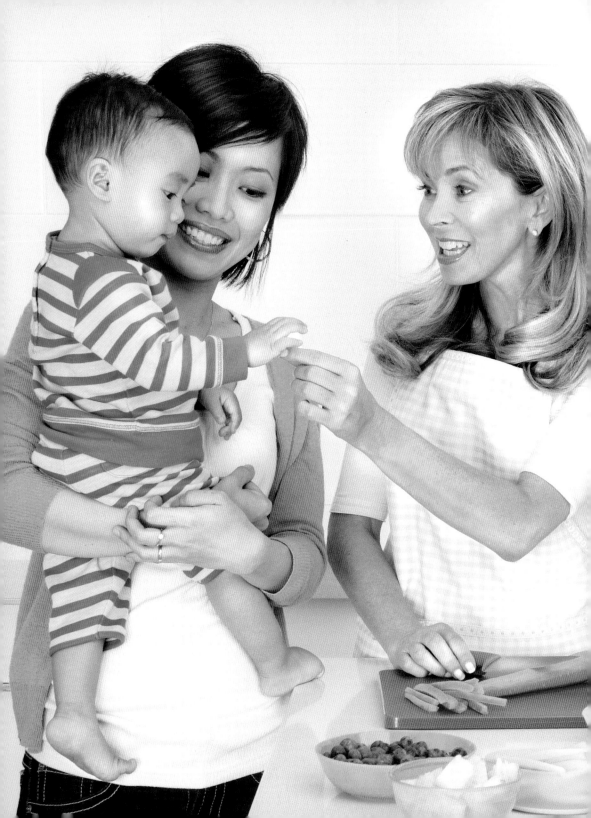

chapter 3

9–12 months:
exploring new tastes

9–12 months:
what you can expect

Your baby will now be showing signs of becoming **an accomplished and self-sufficient eater**. She'll be curious about food, and may be willing to **explore new tastes and textures**, particularly when the rest of the family are doing the same!

Q Can I let my baby feed herself now?

A It's a good idea to encourage your baby to feed herself, and this will develop a wide range of the skills that will eventually be involved in self-feeding, and other manual activities. However, most little ones are unable to feed themselves properly until they are at least two or three years old, and until that time, they will rely on mum, dad, or carer to ensure that the right amount of food is fed into their mouths.

Q Should I allow my baby to use his hands to eat and play with his food?

A This is an important part of the developmental process of learning to eat and to become accustomed to solid foods, and it should be encouraged. The mess may drive you crazy, but your baby should be allowed to touch and feel his food, and to guide it in the direction of his mouth without admonishment. He'll discover the different textures – the way they feel and taste – and will be interested in uncovering new wonders as he gets a little older.

Q How can I encourage my baby to be a little neater while eating?

A Neatness and babies don't really go together when it comes to food. Try to be patient, and allow her to experiment and explore what's on offer. You can discourage her from throwing food or rubbing her mucky hands on the walls or her high chair by taking away her bowl each time she does this, expressing your disapproval, and making her realize that it is unacceptable. However, normal messiness, which can involve a good proportion of the room as well as her face, hands, bib, and clothing, is acceptable and she will soon outgrow the stage.

Q My baby takes only a little solid food; does it matter yet?

A Solids form an important part of your baby's diet after six months of age. If your baby does not eat a lot of solids, it's worth discussing with your doctor or health visitor to ensure that he is getting all the nutrients he needs for normal growth and development.

Q How can I encourage my baby to try new tastes?

A Encourage your baby to experiment! Allow her to try some tastes from your plate, and give her bits when you are preparing food – to lick, suck, "gum", eat, or smell. The more familiar she becomes with various foods, the more adventurous she will be when it comes to eating a wider variety. Once she has passed the first foods stage, offer something new at every meal – consider each food type "new" until she's decided to accept it.

★ talking the talk

Use the same words over and over while mimicking the action you want your baby to adopt – "eat with your spoon" for example. Within a couple of weeks your baby will understand that the words you say mean something specific and be able to carry out the action you are describing.

breast milk and more

Although your baby's diet will be expanding dramatically over the coming months, his usual milk will remain **a large part of his diet** until he **approaches his first birthday**. It's reassuring to know that if your little one is a slow weaner or a faddy eater, the nutrients in breast milk or formula will help him to **grow and develop**.

Q How much milk should my baby be having at this age?

A Until your baby is at least 12 months old, she will need, at the very minimum, 600ml (1 pint) of formula milk or breast milk every single day. Some babies might need more, particularly if they are heavier and growing quickly. During growth spurts, even more milk may be required, so do try to meet your baby's demands, thereby making sure her body's nutritional needs are met. She'll let you know if she's not getting enough.

Q How much water do babies need?

A If your baby is being breastfed, he will need no extra fluid at all. However, if he's thirsty, by all means offer a little cooled, previously boiled water or some very diluted fruit juice. Bottle-fed babies often need more fluids, but because their food at this stage tends to be quite watery, and is typically based on fruits and vegetables, which have a high liquid content, they really don't need much. You could offer 30–60ml (1–2fl oz) of water two or three times a day, and if he drinks it all, offer more. Try to assess what your baby needs, and then act accordingly. Be sure that your baby is getting enough milk – this provides him with a great deal of liquid (see left).

★ did you know ...

that smoothies are a fantastic way to offer fruit (and vegetables) to babies, as they are effectively purées in a more liquid form? It's important to consider the number of fruits involved – the equivalent of a shot glass is plenty – if you are to avoid upsetting your little one's digestion. Berries, ripe bananas, mangos, grapes, papaya, and pears all provide the basis for a great smoothie. Throw in some cucumber, bell pepper, or carrot juice to increase the nutrient factor.

Q Do I need to stop breastfeeding now that my baby has teeth?

A There is no need to stop breastfeeding as long as both you and your baby enjoy it. While the introduction of teeth can cause a little discomfort in the early days, if your baby tries to use your breast as a teething ring, or accidentally or playfully bites you, if she is latched on correctly, teeth will make no difference to the process. In fact, you can be sure that your nutritious milk is helping to produce even healthier teeth! The World Health Organization suggests that breastfeeding should be continued for two years. This may seem a long time at this point, but it's something to aspire to, if you can manage it.

Q My baby seems to think it's funny to bite me; what can I do?

A Babies love to experiment with their new skills and tools, and may realize that they get an instant reaction by using their teeth to best effect. Making mummy shriek may seem very amusing, but it's important that you lay down the law early on, or you will have very sore breasts, and your baby may find that his nursing days are over. Say "no" very firmly when your baby bites you, and remove him from the breast. He may become distressed, and want to return. That's fine, but if he does it again, remove him and leave it for longer. He'll soon learn that he won't get his usual feed if he nips. Try to wait until your baby is hungry before offering him a feed. A hungry baby will not usually bother with games. If he's in a playful mood and just wants a little comfort, amuse him with games, stories, and songs instead, or offer a cuddle. Babies are more likely to bite if they aren't fully engaged in feeding, so some pre-emptive action might save you from a little pain.

Q Do I need to breastfeed for longer if my baby seems to suffer from reactions to food?

A There is quite a lot of evidence to suggest that long-term breastfeeding does offer some protection from allergies. It is, however, very important that your diet does not contain any of the foods that are considered to be problematic, and you will be able to establish exactly what these foods are only with the help of an allergy specialist (see page 58). In the short and long term, however, you will be offering your baby your own antibodies through breastfeeding, which will help to prop up her immature immune system. So, offering your baby breast milk for longer will ensure that she gets the nutrients, calories, and antibodies she needs to grow and develop properly, and minimize the risk of allergies.

Q Can a drink of juice or another snack take the place of a feed when I am weaning?

A No, babies do need their regular milk to provide them with the right calories and nutrients for growth and development. You may find that your baby is hungry or thirsty between feeds and meals, at which point it is fine to offer an extra drink or a healthy snack. If it's close to a mealtime, try to stave her off, so that she will eat enough healthy food to keep her going.

fun with finger foods

Finger foods are a wonderful way to introduce your baby to various **tastes and textures,** and will help to encourage independent eating. Your baby will enjoy **the process of feeding himself** as well as **the new variety of foods** that you offer. The more you encourage this process, the easier the transition will be.

Q How do we progress from purées to lumps?

A The simple answer is a little at a time. All babies develop at different paces, but by now your baby should be a confident purée eater, and will probably have mastered some finger foods. Not all babies find the transition easy, and some actively avoid lumps for as long as they can. Try to stay calm and work at your baby's pace.

You can begin by mashing rather than puréeing some of her favourite foods, as these will be familiar to her, and she'll find the process less daunting. You can also try adding a few of her usual finger foods to her purées – some toast fingers alongside her puréed vegetables, or some mini pasta shapes stirred into her broccoli with cheese. Let her get used to every stage before rushing her on. You are much better off letting her explore mashed foods for a few weeks before moving to finely chopped.

Q How can I tell if my baby is ready for finger foods?

A There are two schools of thought about this one. Some people believe that finger foods should be offered first, and in many cases instead of purées. Others believe that purées should be offered first, and when babies are developmentally ready to pick up, bite, chew, and swallow finger foods, they can be offered – somewhere after nine months. Personally, I think that there is no reason why the two approaches can't be combined. If your baby is a confident eater, offering a variety of finger foods alongside purées is a good way to accustom him to different textures and tastes, and also encourages him to learn the basics of self-feeding. Babies naturally begin to pick things up and explore them, inevitably putting them into their mouths, at around five or six months. From this point on, offering food instead of a toy can provide a nice introduction to the exciting world of food! Be careful what you choose: your baby should be able to gnaw the food without choking or gagging, and be able to derive enough taste by working on it with his gums or budding teeth. Always supervise your baby when he is eating finger food, no matter what his age.

Q How do I introduce finger foods?

A I would suggest offering finger foods at every mealtime, alongside your baby's normal purées, but only after you have established several different fruits, vegetables, and other foods that have been successfully introduced, without any adverse reactions or effects. I've also found that it's useful to have a bowl with several different compartments for holding a range of different finger foods.

Offering finger foods does help to teach your baby to feed herself, and to increase her food repertoire a little. If she picks something up and tastes it, she may not like it to begin with or for the first few times she tries it, but eventually she may consider it to be familiar enough to eat.

Q Which are the best first finger foods for my baby?

A The very same finger foods that we suggested in the previous chapter are also appropriate here (see page 61). Go for easy-to-manage pieces of fruits (melon, apple, banana, kiwi fruit), lightly steamed vegetables (carrot, broccoli, green beans), little sandwiches with healthy fillings, rice cakes, small chunks of cheese, hard-boiled egg, healthy wholemeal breakfast cereals, berries, dried fruits, well-cooked pasta shapes, toast fingers, and the like. Choose brightly coloured fruits for their enhanced nutritional value, and wholemeal goodies over those that have been refined. You can even offer foods such as my delicious fish goujons (see page 138), chicken meatballs, without the sauce (see page 216), which your baby can taste, suck, and gnaw at, or pieces of chicken, which will serve the same purpose.

Q My baby won't try any of the finger foods I've offered! How can I encourage him to eat them?

A Don't panic! Some babies are slow starters, and may well need a little encouragement to pick up food, move it round their mouths, and then swallow. It's a lot to take on board, and can take a little time. Why not try cutting his foods into fun shapes, such as stars, or use a biscuit cutter to create a cat or a moon? You can also try arranging the finger foods as a picture – a smiley face, perhaps. Some babies find it easier to hold larger pieces, such as a whole carrot. Brightly coloured foods always appeal more to little ones; try topping toast fingers with Red Leicester cheese, and grilling, or offer a selection of fresh fruit chunks with his dry cereal.

★ tempting family food

One good way to encourage your little one to eat foods that are a little chunkier is to offer her food that the whole family is eating, perhaps offering mashed potatoes, a little minestrone soup, or rice mixed with small chunks of chicken. She'll feel very grown up eating what everyone else has on their plates, and may not notice the change in texture.

PREPARATION TIME 5 MINUTES | COOKING TIME 20 MINUTES | MAKES 2 BABY PORTIONS

oven-baked sweet potato wedges

These sweet potato wedges are **a tasty and healthy alternative** to chips. **I have left the skin on** the potato as it contains a lot of extra vitamins and fibre. To vary, sprinkle on some Parmesan; or, for babies over a year, **make the wedges spicy**. They are good served with a soured cream and chive dip.

1 small sweet potato, scrubbed

2 tsp olive oil

1 tbsp finely grated Parmesan (optional)

For older babies (optional)

Salt and pepper and a good pinch of paprika

Or a good pinch of fajita seasoning

1 Preheat the oven to 200°C (180°C fan), gas 6.

2 Cut the potato lengthways into about eight wedges. Put the oil in a bowl, add the wedges, and toss to coat. For babies over one, season with a little salt and pepper and the paprika, or the fajita seasoning, if using.

3 Lay the wedges on a baking sheet lined with baking parchment, spacing them out. Bake for about 10 minutes, then turn them over and bake for another 10 minutes or until tender. If you are not using the spices, you can sprinkle the wedges with the Parmesan, then bake for 1 minute.

4 Cool slightly before serving. Once cooled completely, the wedges can be stored in the fridge for 1 day. Reheat in a dry non-stick frying pan for 2–3 minutes, turning once.

sandwich ideas

Finger sandwiches are **good for children of all ages**, for lunch or a snack. **I like to flatten the bread** – this does make a difference for small children as they get a better ratio of filling to bread, and the sandwiches are **suited to little mouths.** Keep fillings fairly smooth.

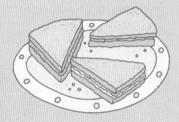

maple-banana sandwich

★ Spread 1 tsp maple syrup over one slice of bread, then top with ½ small mashed banana. Sandwich with the second slice of bread.

avocado sandwich

★ Mash ¼ small, ripe avocado with a few drops of lemon juice. Spread over one slice of bread and sandwich with the second slice.
Variation: You could also try mixing avocado with cream cheese and chopped tomato.

cream cheese-strawberry sandwich

★ Mix 1 tbsp cream cheese with 1 tsp fruit spread or low-sugar spread. Spread over one slice of bread and sandwich with the second slice.

cheese sandwich

★ Spread the bread with a little margarine, cover with a slice of Swiss cheese, and top with the second slice of bread.
Variation: Try adding a couple of thin slices of peeled cucumber or tomato.

PREPARATION TIME 10 MINUTES | COOKING TIME 45 MINUTES, PLUS PASTA COOKING | MAKES 6 BABY PORTIONS

my first tomato sauce, with pasta stars

Sweet vegetables blended with tomato make a nice early pasta sauce for babies, helping them to **get used to the new texture** of pasta. Small stars or alphabetti are ideal first pastas as they are **easy to swallow.** You could also use couscous.

1 tbsp olive oil

½ small red onion, chopped

¼ small butternut squash, peeled, deseeded, and grated

1 carrot, peeled and grated

400g (14oz) can chopped tomatoes

120ml (4fl oz) vegetable stock or water

1 tbsp tomato purée

1 tsp soft light brown sugar

Pepper

Per portion

1–2 tbsp pasta stars or other small shapes (according to appetite)

1 tbsp grated Cheddar cheese (optional)

1 Heat the oil in a large frying pan or wok and gently sauté the onion, squash, and carrot, stirring, for 3–4 minutes until softened but not browned. Add the tomatoes, stock, tomato purée, and sugar. Bring to the boil, then reduce the heat, part-cover, and simmer for about 40 minutes or until thickened. Season to taste with a little pepper.

2 Cool slightly, then blend to a purée. The sauce can be frozen in individual portions; when needed, thaw for 1 hour at room temperature, or in a microwave for 30–60 seconds.

3 To serve, cook the pasta according to packet instructions. Drain and return to the pan, then stir in the pasta sauce and cheese, if using. Stir until the cheese melts and the sauce is piping hot. Cool slightly before serving.

your baby gourmet

You'll **be amazed by what** your baby will eat. Introduce your little one to new textures and tastes as early and as often as you can, to **establish healthy and diverse eating habits** that he will carry with him into childhood and adult life.

Q Will exotic fruits be too sophisticated for my baby's tastebuds?

A Because most of us were not introduced to exotic foods in childhood, we tend to think of them as being "adult food". However, this is simply not the case. When they are properly ripened, exotic fruits are delicious, easy to digest, and full of all the vitamins and minerals your baby needs. We often underestimate what babies are prepared to eat. They enjoy unusual tastes, and will explore anything that is offered to them in the early days.

I highly recommend putting exotic fruits, such as papaya, melon, mango, kiwi, and passion fruit, firmly on the menu. See my purée recipe on page 102.

If you have an unripe exotic fruit, pop it in a bag with a banana; its enzymes will encourage ripening, or leave it on your windowsill to let the sun work its magic.

Q Should I give my baby only fruits that are in season?

A Most exotic fruits are incredibly sweet and tasty when they are ripe and in season; however, if you get them when they are out of season they can be a huge disappointment. For this reason it's worth eating seasonal, locally grown fruits – they will be tastier, sweeter, more nutritious, and usually less tart than those that have been flown in from other climes, and therefore you baby is more likely to enjoy them.

Q How can I make exotic and other fruits into a treat for my baby?

A There is something to be said for creating a little bit of good press, and playing up the virtues of new foods. If you present a beautifully cut mango with a sprig of mint and some cherries to make it look like a hedgehog, you have created the ideal treat for your baby. If you explain that you are so lucky to have found some figs, passion fruit, papaya, cherries, kiwi, or lychees, and then serve them with a flourish, your little one (and your other children) will be much more impressed.

Q My husband likes to give our little one a taste of what he's eating, including Chinese food and curries. She seems to like it – but is it OK?

A Children are much more adventurous with food than grown-ups often give them credit for. My daughter loved olives at the age of 18 months and when I planned the menu for a chain of nurseries, we found that the children's favourite dish on the menu was chicken curry. There are many styles of cooking from around the world that appeal to children and it's easy to make your own versions of healthy mild curries, stir fries, pasta dishes, and enchiladas, for example. What's more, they provide fantastic opportunities to sneak more vegetables into your baby's diet.

If you're eating out, just little tastes are best at the outset. Look out for whole nuts, which should not feature until your baby is five. Lots of sugar, salt, and MSG (an additive that is commonly used in Chinese and other foods) should also be avoided. Unless there are any particular allergy concerns, you can enjoy introducing your little one to different tastes and cuisines. Stick to foods using ingredients you recognize, and if you aren't sure about what might be included, ask the chef.

Q Strong flavours and spicy foods seem to appeal to my baby. Will they harm his digestion?

A If your baby likes the flavours, and he has no reactions after eating them, then you can happily introduce whatever spices and herbs appeal. In other countries, babies are brought up on very strong, spicy curries and other foods, and cope very well. Indeed, there are properties in many spices that may help to prevent diarrhoea, and encourage the health of your baby's gut.

It's important to avoid salt in spicy food, but, most certainly an adventurous nine-month-old should enjoy foods with strong flavours and a hint of spice without any problem. See my Chicken and apricot curry recipe on page 103, which contains just a hint of spice to tempt your little one. This can be adapted for the whole family – just add as much spice as you can handle to the rest of the curry.

★ **did you know ...**

that you can add wine, which offers a rich, lovely flavour, to many of the dishes you prepare for your baby? What you must do, however, is ensure that it is sufficiently boiled (or even simmered) for at least 10 minutes, as this causes the acohol content to evaporate and the flavour to remain. For example, chicken and fish can be poached in wine, and tougher cuts of meat, used in stews and casseroles, can be slow-cooked in wine to tenderize and provide flavour.

PREPARATION TIME 3 MINUTES | MAKES 1 BABY PORTION

banana and mango or peach

Exotic fruits such as **mango, peach, papaya, melon, and kiwi** are perfect baby foods and they don't need any cooking. Introduce them by **mixing with banana**. For older babies, a wedge of peeled mango, melon, or kiwi fruit will **make good finger foods**. All of these fruits are very nutritious.

1 small, ripe banana

½ small, ripe mango or 1 ripe peach

1 Peel the banana and mango or peach (for how to peel a peach, see page 80).

2 Mash the fruits together until quite smooth. (This purée is not suitable for freezing.)

PREPARATION TIME 10 MINUTES | COOKING TIME 30 MINUTES | MAKES 2–3 BABY PORTIONS

chicken and apricot curry

While a very hot curry may **not hit the spot for babies**, a mild and **creamy one is often popular**. This recipe is a good way to tempt your baby to try **more exciting foods from an early age.**

1 tsp sunflower oil

1 small shallot, finely chopped

2 tsp korma or mild curry paste
  (or to taste)

200ml (7fl oz) coconut milk
  (or ½ x 400g/14 oz can)

4 ready-to-eat dried apricots, chopped

1 skinless, boneless chicken breast,
  or 2 skinless, boneless chicken thighs,
  cut into small cubes

To serve

Cooked white rice or couscous

1 Heat the oil in a saucepan and sauté the shallot very gently for 1 minute to soften. Add the curry paste and cook gently for 30 seconds, stirring. Stir in the coconut milk and apricots. Bring to the boil, then reduce the heat and simmer for about 5 minutes or until the apricots start to soften.

2 Add the chicken and stir well, then part-cover and simmer, stirring occasionally, for about 20 minutes or until the chicken and apricots are both tender and the sauce is reduced and thick.

3 The curry is quite soft and so is "gummable", but you can mash or purée it to your baby's preferred consistency. Allow to cool slightly and serve warm, with rice or couscous.

4 The curry can be frozen in individual portions; thaw overnight in the fridge when needed. Add 1 tsp water per portion and heat until piping hot in the microwave or in a saucepan. Cool slightly and check the temperature before serving.

babies on special diets

Whether your baby has a special diet for religious or cultural reasons, lifestyle choices, or food allergies, **it is possible to offer diverse and healthy food** with all of the important nutrients. Babies have slightly **different needs to adults**, so if there are foods you wish to avoid, it's a good idea to get advice from a qualified dietitian.

Q Can my baby get all the nutrients she needs from a vegetarian diet?

A If your baby is on a follow-on formula, you do not need to be worried about nutrients in her vegetarian diet. It is, however, good practice to ensure that she begins to eat plenty of iron and vitamin B12-rich foods, and this is essential if your baby is breastfed. If your family eats eggs, shellfish, or fish, this can be a good way to top up levels; otherwise look for fortified cereals or soya products, which have the vitamin added. Good levels of iron are found in leafy greens as well as dried fruits, chickpeas, and baked beans. Your baby will also require additional vitamin D, but fortunately many products are fortified with this key vitamin; spending time outside in the sunlight will also help.

Q Are fruit and vegetables alone sufficient for my baby?

A Fruit and vegetables offer an amazing number of nutrients, including vitamins and minerals. They don't, in general, offer much in terms of fat, protein, iron, or calcium, and these food groups are very important for growth and development. It's a good idea to mix vegetables with a cheese sauce.

While your baby's regular milk will supply him with the missing bits of his diet in the short-term, he will need much more than fruit and vegetables when he is eventually weaned from his milk diet at around 12–18 months.

Q Are there any vegetables that are not appropriate for babies?

A Some babies have difficulties with onions, cabbage, garlic, and other "wind"-inducing vegetables, but small amounts are often acceptable and this is a problem that is usually resolved within a few months. Deadly nightshade vegetables, such as peppers and aubergines, can sometimes cause discomfort, but this is rare, and it's worth persevering unless she experiences worrying symptoms.

Q What do I need to add to my baby's vegan diet to be sure he's getting enough nutrients?

A If your baby is on follow-on formula, there is no need for concern. However, if you're breastfeeding your baby, you need to ensure he has plenty of iron and vitamin B12 in his diet (see advice on vegetarian diets, left), as well as a vitamin D supplement.

It is a good idea to introduce him to the foods that will become a big part of his diet, such as pulses, leafy green vegetables, soya proteins, and whole grains so that they become familiar and acceptable. It's also important to introduce seeds and nuts (the latter in "butter" form, to prevent choking), to add essential nutrients and protein to your baby's diet. There has been a lot in the news lately about vegan babies failing to grow and develop properly, so you may want to seek some specialist help from a dietitian to ensure that your baby's needs are met.

Q Is wild or brown rice appropriate for babies at this stage?

A Your baby's digestive system is still quite immature, and can struggle with foods that are very high in fibre, such as wild or brown rice, and other whole grains. That doesn't mean they can't be introduced, it simply means that they should be offered in moderation. In the early days, it is a good idea to purée or grind them so that they can be more easily digested. Offer them with protein, such as your baby's usual milk, or a little cheese, butter, or yogurt, as these can slow down their transit through the digestive system, and give your baby's body more time to digest them. They are both nutritious wholegrains, and a couple of tablespoons every few days, is fine.

★ grind some seeds

Ground seeds are a good addition to your baby's diet as they are a great source of protein and they will provide important essential fatty acids to aid your baby's growth, and her neural and brain development. Add them to any purée for extra flavour and texture, or dot them on toast fingers or rice cakes for added crunch and nutrition.

Q My baby has an allergy to fish. How can we be sure she gets EFAs?

A Essential fatty acids (EFAs) are crucial for brain and nervous system growth and development, and there is some evidence to suggest that they affect infants' concentration and mood (see page 203).

Oily fish is the best source of EFAs, but if your baby is allergic to fish, the next best thing is to use seeds and their oils. You can "lace" your baby's meals with natural oils, such as hempseed flaxseed (linseed), and even pumpkin, sesame, and sunflower seed oils. Drizzle some into her smoothies, or onto pasta, or mix it into a dip for her lightly steamed vegetable crudités. You can also buy eggs that are rich in omega-3s, as the hens are fed a special diet that includes oil-rich seeds. A well-cooked scrambled egg made from these provides a source of EFAs.

PREPARATION TIME 5 MINUTES | COOKING TIME 25 MINUTES | MAKES 4–5 BABY PORTIONS

red lentils with carrot and tomato

Carrots are a **good source of antioxidants**, and tomatoes contain lycopene, which is also a strong antioxidant. Quick-cooking red lentils are a good **source of folate, fibre, and iron**, so all together these ingredients make a power-packed orange purée.

1 tbsp sunflower oil

2 large tomatoes, skinned (see page 79), deseeded, and chopped

2 carrots, grated

¼ tsp ground coriander

¼ tsp ground cumin (optional)

115g (4oz) red lentils

200ml (7fl oz) coconut milk (or ½ x 400g/14 oz can)

300ml (10fl oz) vegetable stock, or water

1 Heat the oil in a saucepan and sauté the tomatoes and carrots gently, stirring, for about 5 minutes or until softened. Stir in the coriander and cumin, if using, and cook for 30 seconds. Add the lentils, coconut milk, and stock and stir well to mix.

2 Bring to the boil, then reduce the heat, cover, and simmer very gently, stirring occasionally, for about 20 minutes or until the lentils are soft. Add 1–2 tbsp water if the mix gets too dry during cooking.

3 Cool slightly, then transfer to a blender and blend to a purée. Alternatively, mash to the desired consistency. Serve warm.

4 The purée can be frozen in individual portions; when needed, thaw for about 1 hour at room temperature, or about 1 minute in the microwave on Medium Low, then reheat until piping hot. Stir and allow to cool slightly before serving.

healthy family habits

One of the best ways to introduce your baby to a variety of healthy foods and to **discourage faddy eating** is to encourage her to eat family food. So pull up her chair, and **start encouraging healthy eating** alongside the whole family.

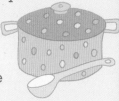

Q **Does it matter if my baby has tastes of foods that aren't recommended until later – such as a little of my breakfast toast with butter, or ice-cream?**

A It is now believed that there is no value in delaying the introduction of allergenic foods beyond six months (see page 46). Unless your little one has in the past shown a reaction to butter, milk, and all dairy produce, as well as eggs, meat, and nuts, these foods can be introduced to your baby from around six months onwards.

The most important thing is that your baby is given something on which he won't choke, and that it is nutritious and healthy. Ice-cream is not particularly healthy, unless you choose good-quality dairy brands, which may prove too rich for your baby, and are also very high in sugar. You can make healthier alternatives; freeze bananas (see page 119), make fresh fruit ice lollies (see page 116), or add fruit purée to plain yogurt.

Q **Are there any staple foods that you would recommend we take with us when we go on a family holiday?**

A It's always difficult to know what might be available when you visit different countries, and it can help to have a few tried-and-tested, healthy food options to hand, particularly if you have access to a kitchen.

Rice and baby rice, as well as small pasta shapes, are a good start, because you can blend them with local fruits and vegetables to provide a nutritious and substantial meal. Look out for good-quality breads, and offer these with some dried fruit, fruit juice, local cheeses (as long as they are pasteurized), yogurt, and even nice cuts of meat or fish.

Sometimes little ones can be fussy, so if your baby has a favourite purée, bring it along in sachet or jarred form to save trouble if your baby refuses local foods. A few finger foods, such as rice cakes, boxes of dried fruits, and even healthy "snacks", such as carrot or tomato snacks (usually found in the organic baby section), can help to eke things out if your baby really doesn't like the taste of something she is offered. However, at the same time, use your holiday to introduce her to new foods, and try to encourage her to try new things.

Q Is it too early to teach table manners?

A Babies can learn rudimentary table manners, such as washing their hands before eating (part of the pre-dinner routine), sitting in their seats until the meal has finished (no more than 20 minutes for youngsters, or you will have a battle on your hands), and not throwing their food. That isn't to say that they will adopt these "manners" instantly, but with constant repetition and reinforcement they will become a habit.

Q My parents are continually offering "junk" food to my baby; how can I persuade them not to, particularly when he likes them?

A Unfortunately, many foods that are considered to be "treats" also fall into the junk food category. Your parents are simply trying to please your baby, and to give him what they think will make him happy, and there is nothing wrong with that in principle. What you need to do is to explain that your baby is perfectly happy with healthy alternatives, such as rice cakes, dried fruits, yogurts, cheese, and home-made biscuits, for example. If he doesn't develop a taste for sweet, fatty, or salty foods in the early years, he'll be less likely to demand them later on.

You could mention the fact that children offered inappropriate foods in the early days are more likely to develop unhealthy eating patterns that can lead to them being overweight. You could also save a few "healthy" treats to be offered only during periods when grandparents are around, making them that much more special. Try not to be too hard on your parents, though. If they see your little one infrequently, the odd naughty snack or meal will do him absolutely no harm.

Q My baby wants crisps, biscuits, and sweets like her older siblings; how can I avoid giving in?

A The best advice is to make sure that your whole family is eating healthy foods. This may sound a bit extreme, but if the older ones become accustomed to choosing fruits, wholemeal biscuits, rice cakes, cheese and yogurts (for example) as snacks, that is exactly what your little one will consider to be normal. I always believe that you should buy only what you want your children to eat. There is no point in complaining that they always eat crisps and treats if that's what they find in your cupboards. Choose your shopping carefully. Hungry kids will eat what is available, and although they may object at the outset, they will soon develop healthy eating habits.

★ treat time

There is no reason why you can't offer your baby a little of a particular treat, such as a chocolate biscuit, on special occasions, or when your older children are having treats. Perhaps you save dried fruit, a small carton of baby fruit juice, a miniature cheese, or yogurt-coated raisins for outings or other treat times. He'll be satisfied if he thinks he's getting something special.

fads and faves

Some babies are undoubtedly pernickety, choosing the same foods over and over again, and **turning up their noses** at the sight of anything new. **The good news** is that you can still offer a delicious, varied, and healthy diet by using a few **tried and tested tricks** – and, of course, a little subterfuge when necessary!

Q Is it possible to convert a baby who has been fed only baby food from jars?

A Of course it is! Start by throwing away the jars and offering her family meals. For one thing, your baby will feel thrilled to be involved, and she is now old enough to have more or less the same things that everyone else is eating. If she proves to be resistant, you can mix a little bit of her usual jarred food with whatever you are eating, and then gradually change the ratio until she is eating different things. Once she becomes accustomed to different tastes, she'll be less likely to resist what you are offering, and if she feels that she is involved by eating with the family, she'll be unlikely to create a fuss.

If you need to, you can get a little sneaky and fill her jars with your own homemade creations. Start by recreating her favourite jarred foods, and then gradually change them until you have her eating what you want.

Q How can I prevent my baby from developing a sweet tooth?

A It's sometimes hard, but try to avoid offering your baby anything with added sugar, and make sure that his meals are based around vegetables rather than fruit, which are naturally sweeter. Try also to offer fruit purées only when she has had her fill of the vegetable purées.

Q My baby won't eat anything but fruit and "sweet" vegetables. Could she already have a sweet tooth?

A Yes, babies quickly develop a sweet tooth, and, ironically, breastfed babies seem to develop one more quickly because breast milk is naturally sweet, and, really rather delicious! The best thing to do is to start introducing less sweet fruits, such as tart apples and berries, and then mix them with your baby's normal food. You can also start to blend together some less sweet vegetables, such as courgettes, broccoli, cabbage, and kale with your baby's sweeter vegetable purées.

A little at a time works well, and she will soon forget the original sweetness that attracted her in the first place.

Q Is there any way to make vegetables more appealing for babies?

A The good news is that babies don't actually dislike vegetables in the same way that toddlers do! If they become accustomed to eating them regularly, and from an early age, they will develop a taste for them. This is one reason why it's a good idea to introduce vegetable purées and finger foods well before you offer the fruity options, and most certainly at the beginning of the meal.

If your baby has always been resistant to vegetables, try blending them with a little fruit to make them more palatable. And at the outset, offer some of the more naturally sweet options, such as sweet potato, squash, and peas. Cubes of these make excellent and nutritious finger foods, too, and will encourage your baby to experiment with different textures.

You can add a little cow's milk in your cooking, as well as yogurt, cheese, herbs, spices, little bits of meat, and pulses to prepare delicious vegetable-based meals. If it's the texture that puts him off, purée the vegetables into sauces, for example a bolognese or tomato sauce (see page 98), and combine with tiny pasta shapes, couscous or rice. Try giving him raw vegetables too.

Q My baby doesn't like fish. Is it very important?

A Fish is important for a number of reasons. It offers a fantastic source of protein, and oily fish in particular (such as fresh tuna, mackerel, salmon, and sardines) has very high levels of EFAs (essential fatty acids), which are required for optimum growth and development, especially visual and brain development.

It may be that your baby doesn't like the particular fish you have chosen. Why not start with something simple like cod or haddock, and mash a couple of teaspoons of poached fish into some mashed potatoes? Salmon can be mixed with mashed potato, some finely chopped spring onion, and a little tomato ketchup to make tasty mini fish cakes. Or make goujons of fish (see page 138). They're simple to make and are great finger foods.

Just keep on offering fish in different guises, and hide it if you need to. It's very important!

☆ did you know ...

that the majority of babies will object when their familiar foods are replaced by something different? It's important to recognize that this is completely normal. Offer her the foods she likes alongside new ones and continue to do so. It can take many "sightings" before your baby will recognize a new food as being familiar. You can blend new and familiar foods together, to accustom her to the taste. Try different combinations of foods or different recipes.

PREPARATION TIME 5 MINUTES | COOKING TIME 10 MINUTES | MAKES ABOUT 6 BABY PORTIONS

salmon, carrot, and peas with cheddar

Salmon is a **very nutritious fish,** but it has quite a strong flavour that your baby might not like at a first try. **Mixing it with potato and carrot will** make it seem more familiar.

150ml (5fl oz) vegetable stock, or water

½ potato, peeled and cut in small dice

1 carrot, peeled and cut in small dice

115g (4oz) skinless, boneless salmon
fillet, cut into 1cm (½in) cubes

2 tbsp frozen peas (preferably petit pois)

30g (1oz) mild Cheddar cheese, grated

1–2 tbsp breast milk or formula

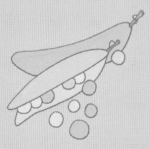

1 Put the stock in a saucepan with the potato and carrot. Bring to the boil, then reduce the heat, cover, and simmer gently for about 6 minutes or until the potato and carrot are just tender.

2 Add the salmon and peas, cover again, and simmer for 3–4 minutes until the fish flakes easily and all the vegetables are tender.

3 Transfer the contents of the saucepan to a bowl and add the grated cheese. Mash to the desired consistency, adding a little breast milk or formula, if necessary. The mixture can also be blended to a purée if your baby prefers a smooth texture.

4 Cool as quickly as possible, then cover and chill. This can be frozen in individual portions; thaw overnight in the fridge, then reheat until piping hot. Stir and allow to cool slightly before serving.

keeping your baby healthy

Your baby's diet will **impact on his health** and affect his mood, energy levels, and sleeping patterns too. Ensuring that he is eating well will go a long way towards **encouraging optimum health**. And when he does fall ill, there is plenty you can do to help him to **recover quickly and easily**.

Q **My baby seems quite hyper after some meals; what foods might be causing this?**

A Refined carbohydrates, such as white pasta, rice, and flour, as well as sugar, can cause your baby's blood sugar to rise quite suddenly, giving him a burst of energy that quickly dissipates into exhaustion and sometimes tearfulness. If this is a regular pattern, swap his refined carbs for wholegrains, choosing wholewheat pasta and bread over the white alternatives, and brown rice and wholewheat flour instead.

Cut out the sugar, too. Sometimes your baby will appear to be a little hyperactive after a big glass of fruit juice or a meal that contains a lot of sweet fruits or vegetables. These are healthy foods, so you can try adding a little protein alongside, such as some yogurt, cheese, chicken, fish, lentils, chickpeas, or even a bit of his usual milk, to prevent them from hitting his bloodstream with a rush of sugar.

Q **My baby is teething and won't eat; is there anything that will soothe her?**

A Try not to worry. Illness and teething can have a huge impact on your baby's appetite, and in the short term this will cause no problems. Foods that require some chewing may make her more uncomfortable, so it might help to revert to smoother purées for a short period, and to offer fresh fruit ice lollies (see page 116) to relieve her symptoms. Offer a teething ring or a cold, clean wet flannel for her to chew on in advance of meals, as this can remove the worst of the discomfort.

Q **Is there anything I can do for my baby's constipation?**

A In most cases, constipation is the result of inadequate fluid and/or fibre in your baby's diet. Encourage him to drink plenty of water throughout the day, and ensure that he gets lots of fresh fruit and vegetables in his diet, which are a good source of both fluids and fibre. Water-rich finger foods, such as papaya, melon, mango, quartered grapes, and red pepper strips, are ideal choices. Consider, too, giving him a little wholemeal bread, brown rice, and other wholegrains, which are high in healthy fibre.

Q What is the difference between probiotics and prebiotics and why do so many baby foods contain them?

A Probiotics are essentially strains of healthy bacteria that are introduced to your baby's diet, so that they can settle in the gut and establish a healthy "colony" to combat the unhealthy bacteria and other "invaders", such as viruses or fungi, which may try to take over. They remain intact throughout the digestive process, and deliver healthy bacteria directly to the large intestine. Your baby's gut forms an important part of her immune system, and having a good, healthy balance of "flora" (healthy bacteria), plays an important part in keeping illness at bay. You'll find them naturally in live yogurt, and they are added to different foods.

Prebiotics are non-digestible food ingredients that encourage your baby's own healthy bacteria (flora) to grow in her gut. Natural prebiotics include asparagus, garlic, leeks, onions, and artichokes, but because these are not the usual baby fare, prebiotics are often added to formula, cereals, and other food to ensure that your baby gets what she needs for optimum immunity.

Q Are there any foods that I should avoid when my baby has a vomiting and diarrhoea virus?

A Continue to offer milk feeds regularly, with extra rehydration solution and water, if necessary (see page 37). Citrus fruit, fruit juices, and strong spices all seem to have a negative impact on the digestive system, and can make symptoms worse. Stick to the basics, and offer rice, ripe bananas, apples, as well as a little toast. These foods will help to keep up your baby's energy levels.

★ allergy alert

If you believe that food is causing symptoms, or making your baby unwell in any way (see pages 57–58 for a list of possible symptoms) then you should see your doctor, who may wish to refer you to a specialist, who can work out if there are any allergies or intolerances afoot. See page 58 for more information on diagnosing food allergies.

Q Is there any truth in the saying "feed a cold and starve a fever"?

A In both cases it is important to ensure that your baby is getting enough fluids, as dehydration is far more serious than any fever or cold. Some babies (and adults!) do seem to go off food when they have a temperature, which is probably the body's natural reaction, as it diverts energy away from the digestive system towards the areas that need healing.

In the case of a cold, which is usually more superficial, babies might be hungrier, as they require nutrients to fight off the infection, and don't have one particular part of the body demanding attention. The best advice is to follow your instincts. If your baby is hungry, offer him something to eat; if he isn't, give him plenty to drink. If there is no resolution or change within 48 hours, pay a visit to your doctor.

PREPARATION TIME: 5 MINUTES | MAKES 6–8 LOLLIES

peach melba lollies

Fresh fruit ice lollies are **great for soothing sore gums** when your **little one is teething**. They are also a great way to get more fluids into your sick child. This is a lovely combination of fruits, but these would also be **tasty made with peaches and strawberries**.

2 large, ripe peaches

175g (6oz) fresh or frozen raspberries (or you could use strawberries)

300ml (10fl oz) peach or apple juice

2–3 tbsp caster sugar (optional)

1 Peel the peaches (see page 80), then quarter them and remove the stones. Put the peaches and berries in a blender with half the juice and blend to a purée. Pass the purée through a sieve to remove the seeds.

2 Mix the purée with the remaining peach or apple juice and sweeten to taste with sugar, if needed.

3 Pour the purée into lolly moulds and freeze for a few hours or overnight.

healthy weight gain

It's natural to become preoccupied with your baby's weight, veering between concerns that **your baby is overweight** and worrying that he's not **growing at the right pace.** The good news is that a healthy, balanced diet will ensure he hits and maintains just the right weight for him, setting him in **good stead for the years to come.**

Q Is there any way to prevent my baby from becoming overweight?

A Breastfeeding is the most effective way to prevent babies becoming overweight, as breastfed babies are much less likely to develop problems with obesity in later life. If you are beyond this point, then watch how and when you are feeding your baby. You should offer her the milk she needs, but watch for cues that she is full, and then stop. Don't try to feed her up in the hope that she will sleep better, or last longer between feeds.

Similarly, never ask her to clear her plate. Give her tastes of everything on offer, and when she says no more, stop feeding her. Be careful, too, about offering milk or food as a comfort when your baby is upset. While it can be an easy way to soothe her, she will soon learn to associate food with comfort, which can eventually lead to comfort eating and obesity. Offer healthy snacks (see page 78) when she is hungry, to keep her blood sugar levels stable, and prevent cravings.

Finally, base her diet around fresh, whole foods, with plenty of fruit and vegetables, and lots of lean proteins such as lentils, fish, chicken, and beef. With a full tummy she's unlikely to demand extra snacks.

Q How can I tell if my baby is overweight?

A To every parent their baby looks perfect, no matter what his size. In fact, studies have indicated that parents are often the last people to recognize a weight problem in children. Yet, a healthy baby may look plump and chubby, and this is no bad thing.

Unless your baby has jumped a couple of centile lines on his growth chart, which gives you an idea of the weight that is most appropriate for his height and age, you should not be unduly concerned. Some babies are heavily set; others put on weight before a growth spurt or seem a little chubby in advance of developmental stages, when new spurts of activity, such as crawling, even everything out. If your baby is wearing clothes that are larger than his age, or struggling to crawl, bend, or reach because of his size, there may be problems. If you are concerned, talk to your doctor.

Q My baby never seems to be full, and will eat endless quantities of whatever I prepare. Should I stop her?

A It's interesting that some babies have a very strong "full" cue, and will not eat more than they need, while others appear to be able to eat indefinitely. The most important thing to remember is not to coerce your baby into finishing her "meal" when she is clearly not interested. Sometimes your baby may be hungrier than others; sometimes you may need to persuade her to have just a couple of tastes. But when she says no, you must respect that.

If your baby is eating a lot, but still putting on the normal amount of weight for her height (you can check this on her growth chart; see page 34), she may just be growing quickly, or be very active, and in need of more calories for energy. If she's putting on weight, that's another matter, and it's worth paying a visit to your doctor to see if there is any obvious reason for her huge appetite.

Q Should I use reduced fat ingredients?

A First and foremost, babies need fat for a number of important body functions, and you will do her no favours by cutting it out (see page 155). The key is to choose healthy fats (which are liquid at room temperature, and include foods such as olive and vegetable oils) over unhealthy fats (which are hard at room temperature).

Secondly, reduced-fat foods tend to have extra chemicals added to them to make them more appealing or to improve the texture. In many cases, there are a lot of extra sugars or artificial flavours added. In reality, your baby is far better off eating a little of the real thing, than an alternative that is far less healthy.

Q What should I add to my baby's diet if he isn't gaining weight?

A Stir in some egg, milk, cream, cheese, soya, nut butters, ground seeds, and anything that can offer a few more calories without compromising your baby's health. Fattening and unhealthy cakes, biscuits, and other processed foods might help him to gain weight, but they add no nutrition to his diet, and may make him unhealthy in the long-run.

You are far better off choosing good-quality fats and proteins to add to his diet. Drizzle some olive oil over his bread or pasta, or stir it into his purées. Offer some extra healthy snacks to entice him to eat, and to stimulate his appetite (see page 78 for snack ideas), and offer more protein and fat alongside his regular carbohydrates.

★ snack attack

Babies do not, in the vast majoriy of cases, tend to overeat, so offering your little one a snack between meals, if she has had her fill of milk and still seems to want more, is fine. During periods of intensive growth your baby may be very hungry and want more food to satisfy her. The best thing to do is follow her demands. For healthy snack ideas, see page 78 and the finger foods on page 95.

PREPARATION TIME 1 MINUTE PLUS FREEZING | MAKES 4 BABY PORTIONS

far-too-easy banana ice-cream

This tastes so good that you are not going to believe how easy and quick it is to make. It's also **a fantastic, healthy alternative** to traditional ice-cream. Try it!

4 medium, ripe bananas

1 Peel the bananas, then place them on a tray that can be put into the freezer. Pop them into the freezer and leave for at least 4 hours or overnight.

2 Then simply remove the bananas from the freezer (one at a time if you want to make just one portion), cut into chunks, and whizz in a food processor until smooth.

3 If making in bulk, freeze any leftover ice-cream in a plastic box with lid. Remove a portion and allow it to soften a little before serving.

parties and treats

While healthy food is on the day-to-day menu, there is no reason why that **all-important first birthday** and other special events can't provide an opportunity for a few treats. **And with some tricks** up your sleeve, you can provide party fare that is **nutritious and delicious!**

Q What are appropriate foods for my baby's first birthday party?

A The problem with birthday parties is that you have OPC there, too. What are they? Other People's Children! Some parents are fastidious about what their children eat and will expect you to serve entirely healthy fare. I'm in two minds about this. I do think that it is possible to serve healthy, delicious treats, but I also think that birthday parties and other celebrations should be treated slightly more leniently. There must always be times when we can break the rules and get a good, big sugar rush!

You can create healthy party treats by using a little imagination, and if you present it well, you will make it that much more fun. Think about individual pots of apricot and apple purée; tiny sandwiches (see page 97); mini muffins with a little chocolate; chunks of cheese and grape halves; tiny pizzas on pitta bread, mini bagels or English muffins; chunks of pretty fruits and vegetables with dips; little pots of yogurt; and then a resoundingly delicious cake and some fresh fruit jelly to top it all off. There is no need for any of these to be considered "unhealthy". They are fun, child friendly, and are packed with nutrients as well.

Q Do I need to provide allergen-free foods?

A This is a tricky one. Most allergy specialists are not in favour of "nut-free" schools and events, because they believe that children with allergies are lulled into a false sense of security and believe that everything they eat is safe, when it may well not be the case.

I think it's fair to ask if a child has allergies and to cater for this as much as possible (fresh fruit and vegetables will, for example, rarely present a problem, nor will jelly or purées). But if you take on the responsibility for supplying an allergic child with food, you also set yourself up if there are problems. You can, therefore, suggest a few non-allergenic options, but also ask that the parents bring along their own "safe" food as well. Most parents of children who have allergies will not only advise you of the situation, but usually also offer to bring along their own food.

Q Is there a healthy way to make jelly and cake?

A Jelly can be made with fresh fruit juice, with fruit pieces added for extra nutrition. Smaller guests may struggle, so it might be easier to add half puréed fruit, and half water, to prevent difficulties. You can use wholemeal flour for cakes (although look carefully at the recipe, as substitutions don't always work!)

Try baking a cake with fresh wholesome ingredients, packed with fruit, or even vegetables, such as carrots, sweet potato, or courgettes. For a real surprise that will delight guests of all ages see the Ice-cream birthday cake on the following page.

Q Are babies too young for sweets and other treats?

A If you are offering some cake, and perhaps jelly, as well as some sweet options on the birthday menu, there is no need to offer anything else. One-year-olds are too young for sweets as such, and do not need the extra sugar, as your party feast will provide plenty, in much healthier forms. Most babies of this age will not have been introduced to sweets, and they simply won't miss them.

Q Is it OK to serve fruit juice?

A At your child's first birthday party, the little ones will probably be having all sorts of different treats and may well be very thirsty. Water is best, perhaps offer it in small bottles. A little heavily diluted juice is OK, but don't be tempted to offer anything sweeter. The food is what counts, and keeping the babies hydrated with healthy, fresh water or diluted juice will make it more enjoyable for all.

Q Are there some easy ideas for serving adults?

A For the first few years, adults do accompany their little ones to birthday parties, so it does make sense to offer something. Some crudités with dip; pitta bread with hummus; chicken skewers with peanut sauce (if there are no nut allergies about); mini tarts, or just a platter of delicious cheese with fresh bread, grapes, and ripe tomatoes is perfect.

★ did you know ...

that there are lots of great finger foods you can prepare that are festive and appropriate for babies? Tiny sandwiches (see page 97) are always a good idea, as are breadsticks, little pots of hummus, lightly steamed vegetable crudités, chunks of cheese, toast fingers with jam, and fresh fruit. Raisins, sultanas, and dried apricots are also usually appealing, but it's a nice idea to lightly steam them so they are soft and plump for the less confident chewers.

PREPARATION TIME 30 MINUTES (PLUS 30 MINUTES SOFTENING) | CUTS INTO 12–14 PORTIONS

ice-cream birthday cake

The first birthday party can be a bit of a challenge – expectations will be high. I like to surprise people by **serving an ice-cream cake** rather than the traditional birthday sponge. Your guests will be delighted, and it can be **made a couple of weeks** in advance.

Cake

2 litres (3½ pints) or 4 x 500ml (18fl oz) tubs of good-quality vanilla ice-cream or frozen vanilla yogurt, softened in the fridge for 30 minutes

500ml (18fl oz) tub raspberry sorbet, softened in the fridge for 30 minutes

Raspberry sauce

450g (1lb) fresh, or frozen and thawed, raspberries

150–200g (5½-7oz) good-quality raspberry jam (to taste)

½ tsp lemon juice

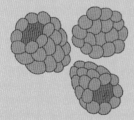

1 Put a 23cm (9in) springform cake tin in the freezer to chill. Spread half of the frozen ice-cream over the bottom of the tin and press down to level. Freeze for 10 minutes to firm up a little, then spread over a layer of sorbet, pressing level again. Freeze for 10 minutes, then top with a level layer of the remaining ice-cream. Wrap the tin tightly in foil and freeze overnight, or until needed.

2 To make the sauce, purée the raspberries with the jam and lemon juice. Sieve to remove any seeds, then cover and chill (can be made a day ahead).

3 About 45 minutes to 1 hour before serving, transfer the cake to the fridge, so it can soften slightly. Undo the spring clips on the side of the tin, lift off the side, and transfer the cake to a plate. Use a large, sharp knife to cut slices, dipping it in very hot water between each slice. Serve with the raspberry sauce spooned over.

★ **Variation:** Substitute strawberry ice-cream for the vanilla ice-cream, and serve with a warm white chocolate sauce made by melting 225g (8oz) white chocolate with 250ml (8fl oz) double cream.

chapter 4

12–18 months:
toddlers on the move

12–18 months:
what you can expect

The **transition from baby to toddler** is an exciting one for both you and your little one, and you'll find he is now capable of eating a wide variety of foods – some of them **all on his own!**

Q **My toddler seems to be using mealtimes to exert her will; how can I prevent this from becoming a problem?**

A Early in life, most children cotton on to the fact that their parents are concerned about how much and what they are eating. Making a fuss about food guarantees instant attention, and many children slide into the habit of using food to wield power over their parents. The best advice is to remove the pressure. If children fail to get a response, they get bored. When they realize that they won't get attention for eating badly, they'll stop using food as a tool to do so.

So, if your toddler won't eat, remove full or half-empty plates without a murmur, after around 30 minutes. Don't offer an alternative, and try not to panic too much that she hasn't eaten enough of the right foods. No child, whatever her age, will willingly starve herself, and if you continue to offer healthy food, with no pressure attached, she will eventually eat it.

Q **Should my toddler be feeding himself by now?**

A Most toddlers will be able to finger feed successfully at 12–18 months. They are very unlikely to manage to eat with cutlery, but they can try! Provide your toddler with his own cutlery, and encourage him to get his fingers messy, and he'll soon learn the necessary skills. The best way to approach this is to encourage him to eat with both his hands or cutlery, while you feed him at the same time. By watching you feed him, he learns the art of picking up a spoon, filling it with food, and placing it in his mouth – he'll soon be doing this himself, once he knows how.

Q **Is it OK for my toddler to eat little but often?**

A Some little ones can't seem to manage much at mealtimes, either because they lack the concentration necessary to sit down and finish a bowl or a plate of food, or because their tummies are small, and it takes very little to fill them up. In this case, it's fine to offer a few small meals, as long as they are all equally healthy, and not junky snacks that will fill them up with empty calories.

Q **Is it necessary for my toddler to use cutlery?**

A Presenting a set of "safe" and child-friendly cutlery at a young age, even if your child doesn't use it, instils the idea that cutlery accompanies mealtimes. Many little ones eat with their hands alone, which is certainly a necessary skill to develop, and perfectly acceptable in toddlerhood, but not something that should be encouraged into the preschool years.

⭐ **tempering tantrums**

Tantrums may become increasingly evident at mealtimes. A good way to bypass these is to offer a few choices in advance, so your toddler feels she has a little control. Perhaps let her choose her bowl or which vegetable she might like.

gentle weaning

Weaning is often a **tricky and emotive period** for toddlers and parents alike, as regular milk feeds are replaced with wholesome, nutritious meals. **Don't rush the process** if you aren't ready. As long as milk isn't forming the main part of your toddler's diet, you can continue to enjoy those **comforting moments**.

Q Is it OK to continue to breastfeed even when my toddler is eating a varied diet?

A There is absolutely no reason why you can't continue to breastfeed as long as both you and your toddler are enjoying it. There is plenty of research to suggest that breast milk continues to offer antibodies well into toddlerhood, which can help build up your little one's resistance to infection.

Breast milk also contains a whole host of vitamins and minerals. It is important, though, that your baby has a healthy balance between breastfeeding and solids. The majority of nutrients at this age should come from food, and not breast milk. Filling up on breast milk can lead to reduced food intake, which may lead to vitamin deficiencies.

Most importantly, perhaps, is that breastfeeding offers emotional nourishment and comfort to your child, and helps to build a healthy mother-child relationship.

Q My toddler shows no desire to stop breastfeeding, but it's starting to get embarrassing. What do you recommend?

A If you are feeling pressured because you are breastfeeding past the point at which many mums give up, try limiting it to morning and evening feeds, when you can feed in private. If you are ready to give up altogether, take it slowly. Start by losing one feed at a time and offer a drink or snack in its place. It can take time, but weaning needs to happen sometime (see page 177 for more tips).

Q Should I stop the night-time bottle?

A It is easy to fall into the habit of offering a night-time bottle because it's comforting. The longer this goes on, the harder it is to stop, and drinking from a bottle at night can play havoc with children's teeth (see page 129). It's a good idea to offer a cup instead. However, if you're finding it hard to get your toddler away from his bottle, gradually water down his evening bottle over a few weeks, until it is virtually tasteless, and encourage other comfort items, such as a favourite toy. See box, right, to ensure he gets his calcium requirements though.

Q My child doesn't seem to like water. How can I make it more appealing?

A If your toddler is used to sweet drinks and milk, water probably does seem boring. Buy her a water bottle, perhaps with her favourite character on it, and keep it topped up throughout the day, so she gets into the habit of drinking whenever she is thirsty. Sometimes offering water with some ice cubes and a straw can make it more fun, too. If this doesn't work, try adding a tiny bit of juice or high-fruit squash and then reducing the flavouring little by little until she's drinking water alone.

Q Does it matter if my child won't drink any milk?

A Lots of children can't or won't drink milk, and grow and develop perfectly well. The most important element of milk is calcium, which is required for healthy bones and teeth. Calcium is found in all dairy produce, so if he's eating yogurt, fromage frais, and cheese, he's probably getting enough. Leafy-green vegetables are also a good source of calcium, and use milk when you can in cooking: in rice pudding, creamy or cheese sauces, or even mashed potatoes or other root vegetables.

Q Should my toddler be drinking her milk from a cup?

A It's a good idea to wean your baby on to a cup by the age of 6–12 months, when the sucking reflex is replaced by an ability to sip and swallow. A cup is less damaging to her teeth as the sucking action when drinking from a bottle causes milk to "swirl" around the mouth, bathing the teeth in the natural sugars that it contains. A cup will also limit her association of milk with comfort, which can sometimes lead to problems with comfort eating and weight problems later on – and also difficulties settling without a bottle. Start by switching the teat on her bottle to a "spout", so that she becomes used to drinking rather than sucking. Then buy a few brightly coloured beakers and ask her to choose the one she'd like to have her milk or water in. If she feels that she's got some power to choose, the disappointment of not having a bottle will soon be forgotten.

★ did you know ...

that children over the age of one should get about 570ml milk (1 pint) a day? Remember, though, that this is to provide the total amount of calcium required, so if your toddler has a yogurt or two, some cheese, and milk on her cereal, she'll need correspondingly less. In fact, a glass of milk a day, plus a yogurt and a small piece of cheese is actually just about right for most toddlers, even though it's tempting to offer more than this.

learning to love food

Your toddler needs plenty of variety and lots of different nutrients from fresh, natural foods. **Encourage your little one** to try new foods regularly, and to enjoy versions of healthy family meals, and she'll soon be on her way to **establishing healthy eating patterns** – and learning to love great food!

Q What does a varied "toddler" diet mean?

A A varied diet includes a variety of different foods. We know that kids need the basics of protein, carbohydrates, fats, and vitamins and minerals, and the best way to ensure that they get what they need is to offer as many different foods as often as possible.

★ mix and match

The wider the range of foods you offer the better. Wheat-based pastas or breads offer a good source of carbohydrates, but also include different forms, such as rice, potatoes, and different grains (buckwheat, oats, etc.) from time to time. Offer vegetarian proteins such as tofu or pulses at one meal, and fish or chicken at the next. Experiment with the whole spectrum of brightly coloured fruit and vegetables, ensuring you toddler gets all the key nutrients she needs.

Q How many servings of carbohydrates does my toddler need each day?

A Try to ensure that every meal has at least one or two servings of carbohydrates, and that your child has at least one or two carb-rich snacks as well. Add a little mashed potato, some couscous, pasta, quinoa, or rice to his main meal, alongside fresh vegetables (which are also rich in carbohydrates). Also offer toast, porridge, or cereal with breakfast, and perhaps some breadsticks and fresh fruit at snacktime. Sandwiches, pasta dishes, risottos, and jacket potatoes are also high in carbohydrates.

Q Are there any grains that are too harsh for my toddler's digestion?

A Wholegrains such as brown rice, wild rice, quinoa, oats, millet, and corn are good sources of protein, carbohydrates, vitamins, minerals, and fibre, and are a great addition to a toddler's diet. It is, however, better to stick to small portions as they are rich in fibre and can fill up little tummies very quickly. Too much fibre increases the speed at which foods are digested, which can lead to inadequate intake of some nutrients.

Q How can I persuade my toddler to eat meat?

A Often it's the texture rather than the taste of the meat that toddlers object to. Minced meat is good for little ones; make sure you choose lean mince. When making dishes such as bolognese or shepherd's pie, I often brown the minced meat and then chop it for a few seconds in a blender, so it has a less lumpy texture. Combining a tasty minced meat with a mashed potato and carrot topping, or mixing it with pasta, are other good ways to make it easier to eat.

You can also encourage your toddler to enjoy eating meat or chicken by making mini meatballs that he can pick up with his fingers. My recipe for Chicken meatballs on page 216 contains sautéed red onion, carrot, and apple, so is very tasty and appealing to little children. These can also be made using minced beef. Also consider adding tiny pieces of meat to pastas or risottos, where they aren't quite so overwhelming.

If your child is still resistant to eating meat, don't despair. Pulses such as chickpeas, butter beans, kidney beans, peas, and lentils can all be added to soups, stews, casseroles, or pasta dishes to provide a good source of protein; they can even be offered on their own, as they are easy for little fingers to manage. Rice and wholegrains, such as barley, wheat, buckwheat, corn, and oats, are also high in protein, as are nut butters or ground nuts, seeds and quinoa, which can be eaten on their own, or added to your child's favourite dish.

A little hummus with some wholegrain toast, for example, is a good protein-based snack. Don't forget, too, that eggs and dairy produce are as high in protein as meat, so a scrambled egg with a little grated cheese will be a perfect high-protein meal.

Q Do toddlers need five servings of fruit and vegetables every day?

A Toddlers need at least five servings of fruit and vegetables a day, but it doesn't need to be as daunting as it sounds! At this age, a serving is roughly what your toddler can hold in her hand. So a couple of grapes, a few pieces of apple, or a tablespoon of sweetcorn or peas will count as one serving. Vegetables blended into pasta sauces, and hidden in dishes such as spinach and ricotta lasagne or butternut squash risotto, are other good ways to get your toddler to eat her veggies. Potato doesn't count, but sweet potato and carrots do, so mash potato with these as a topping for cottage pie.

A handful of berries or dried fruit, such as raisins or apricots, make good snacks, and you can sprinkle porridge or breakfast cereal with fresh berries. A small glass of fruit juice or a smoothie also count as a serving. Homemade fresh fruit ice lollies are another tasty way to get your little one to eat more fruit (see my lolly recipe on page 116).

Brightly coloured fruits and vegetables are best for your child as the pigment contains antioxidants (see page 163), so make sure there is plenty of colour on your child's plate.

Q Why are fruit and vegetables so important?

A It probably goes without saying that fruit and vegetables contain most of the essential vitamins and minerals necessary for your child to grow and develop, and to remain healthy, and full of energy. They contain fibre, which encourages healthy digestion and normal bowel movements, and also antioxidants that are vital for good health, and can prevent many health problems (see page 163). The secret is to go for variety – and plenty of colour – which will ensure your toddler gets the whole spectrum of nutrients she needs. A sweet potato or some butternut squash makes a great alternative to an ordinary jacket potato, and a handful of berries, or a piece of fresh, ripe melon, or mango, can offer a fantastic nutrient boost. If it's bright, it's bound to be healthy! Berries are particularly good as they are rich in vitamin C, which helps us absorb iron from our food.

Q My child eats no fruit or vegetables at all, but drinks a lot of juice. Is this enough for his five servings a day?

A Juice is a good way to get a serving of fruit or vegetables into a faddy eater, but it isn't really enough. For one thing, juice contains no fibre, which is important for healthy digestion and bowel movements. Secondly, even the freshest, pure juices contain high levels of natural sugars, which can not only damage your toddler's teeth and encourage a sweet tooth, but play havoc with his blood sugar levels. What's more, his little tummy may be filled by even small servings of juice, preventing him from eating a healthy, balanced main meal.

If he's keen on juice, I suggest looking for some fresh fruit and vegetable blends, preferably with "bits", which do at least offer a little fibre. Always dilute your toddler's juice, and offer it after he's eaten a meal, when it will add to his overall nutrient intake, keep him hydrated, and help the absorption of iron in his food.

It is, however, a very good idea to work on including vegetables and fruit in his daily diet, even if you have to hide them. For some good ideas, see right.

★ did you know ...

that juicing fruit and vegetables can help to ensure your toddler eats a good variety and might also help her to become accustomed to new tastes while getting a good boost of nutrients at the same time? Try blending carrot and orange, or celery, apple, and cucumber. Apricots, peaches, mango, berries, or pears can add sweetness to red pepper, carrots, or beetroot, and make a nutritous combination of ingredients that your toddler may not consider eating on their own.

Q **My toddler's diet seems to consist of three or four favourites, but these include just two fruits. Is this enough or does she need more variety?**

A Most little ones have particular favourites, and are reluctant to try new foods, particularly in the fruit and vegetable range! If she's eating three or four different fruits and vegetables regularly, it's likely that she will be getting a fairly good range of nutrients. It does, of course, depend on what these are! For example, if she eats only peas, corn, apples, and bananas, she'll be missing out on some of the essential vitamins and minerals – in particular, antioxidants (see page 163) – found in brightly coloured fruits and vegetables. It's worth trying to include more of these whenever possible, even if you have to purée them into soups or pasta dishes until she acquires a taste for them.

Continue to offer a variety of foods at mealtimes. Make food look appealing – how about threading some bite-sized pieces of fruit onto a straw? What's more, it sometimes helps to sneak a new food into a plate of favourites without drawing attention to it. Curiosity or hunger may win out. Also consider offering "tapas"-sized bits of new fruits and vegetables, with a favourite dip (see page 137) to try with them. Serve different fruits and vegetables to the whole family, too, and make a good show of enjoying them. Your little one will want to be part of the fun and may just give them a go.

⭐ **juicy nutrients**

If you're struggling to get fruit into your little one, why not try stirring puréed and finely chopped fruit into sugar-free jelly (replacing half the water content with fruit)? Or freeze an exotic smoothie with a little yogurt and runny honey in ice cube trays for a delicious frozen sorbet.

Q **My toddler doesn't like the consistency of vegetables and fruit. Are purées OK at this age?**

A Many little ones find the crunchy texture difficult to manage, and may even gag on small pieces, particularly if their introduction to "lumps" was later than usual. While it's important to encourage toddlers to develop their chewing and swallowing skills, it is equally important to ensure that they are getting the vitamins and minerals they need. Try cooking food to a slightly softer texture, and mashing rather than puréeing it. Blend his usual purées with some lumpier foods that he loves, such as tiny pasta shapes, and continue to offer tempting fruit and vegetable finger foods too. There's no reason why some of his food can't be puréed, but whizz it for a shorter period of time each time you present it. If your little one continues to gag and object to lumps, it's worth visiting your doctor, to reassure yourself that all is well.

PREPARATION TIME 10 MINUTES | COOKING TIME 15 MINUTES | MAKES 2 CHILD PORTIONS

rainbow pasta

When learning to feed themselves, toddlers can get frustrated with a spoon and fork and **prefer to use their fingers**, so pasta dishes that are not too "slippery" are ideal. This one includes a delicious and **colourful range of vegetables** – you can both have fun identifying the colours as your toddler eats.

85g (3oz) pasta shapes

½ carrot, peeled and cut into matchsticks

2 broccoli florets, cut in small pieces

2 tsp olive oil

½ yellow courgette, halved lengthways and sliced

¼ small red pepper, deseeded and cut into matchsticks

3 tbsp crème fraîche

55g (2oz) Cheddar cheese (medium or mild, according to preference), grated

2 tbsp grated Parmesan cheese

1 Cook the pasta in boiling water according to packet instructions, adding the carrot and broccoli for the last 3 minutes of the cooking time.

2 Meanwhile, heat the oil in a large frying pan or wok and stir-fry the courgette and red pepper for 3–4 minutes until softened and lightly golden.

3 Drain the pasta, carrots, and broccoli and add to the frying pan. Add the crème fraîche and cheeses. Toss everything together over a low heat for about 1 minute to heat the crème fraîche and just melt the cheeses. Serve warm. (This dish is not suitable for reheating.)

independent eating

Finger foods aren't just snacks or incidental additions to your toddler's diet. You can supplement even the faddiest toddler's menu with **appealing goodies** that will both add nutritional value and encourage her to learn the **skills of independent eating.**

Q How can I encourage my child to eat foods with different consistencies?

A Some little ones find the transition from purées to lumps, and then to mashed, chopped, and cut food more difficult than others, and may be reluctant to eat meals that require chewing. In some cases, it comes down to laziness, or it may be that weaning took place a little later than usual.

It is important that you continue to introduce foods with different textures. One of the best ways to do this is to offer what is effectively a balanced selection of finger foods at every meal, so everything he eats must be chewed, with no purées at all. For example, peas, sweet potato cubes, strips of chicken, and chunks of steamed new potatoes, or a pot of rice with fish balls and steamed broccoli. Many children seem to find it easier to move straight on to this "real food", rather than progressing through different textures.

Q How small should I mash or chop foods for my toddler?

A Once your toddler has some teeth, she can manage most soft foods that have been diced, grated, or mashed. In fact even without teeth it is surprising what a set of gums can munch their way through. Certainly by 12 to 18 months, your toddler should be able to enjoy a variety of different finger foods, which can be incorporated into his regular meals. As long as the food isn't too tough, which may be beyond the capabilities of little teeth and gums, small pieces of most foods can be managed easily. If your child gags or has trouble managing diced foods, try making the pieces a little smaller until he's more adept at chewing. I often find it useful to whiz tougher cuts of meat in a grinder for a few seconds, to smooth out some of the lumps and bumps, and make them a little softer for little ones. Use your "ground" meats as a base for any meat dish, including pasta sauces, casseroles, or dishes such as Chicken meatballs (page 216) and Funny-face beef burgers (page 185). You can also try increasing the chunks in the foods that he already loves and is most familiar with, where they will not be so readily noticed or identified!

Q My toddler still refuses to eat anything with lumps – what can I do?

A Some babies and toddlers, particularly those who have been weaned onto jarred baby foods, tend to like things smooth! They can often develop the most amazing ability to filter out every single lump and spit them out. Some little ones simply gag because it's taken them a little longer to develop the knack of chewing things well enough to make them easily swallowed. You should visit your doctor, however, if your toddler regularly gags or refuses lumps, as there may be a physical cause at the root.

There are a few ways you can help your child to accept lumpy food. First of all, don't force it. If your toddler senses that you are angry or anxious, he'll begin to find the whole experience of eating traumatic, and may literally gag or choke on even the tiniest lumps because he feels under pressure.

Slowly increase the lumpiness of his food, and allow him to play messily with it. Babies and toddlers tend to prefer overall lumpiness to something smooth with the occasional lump, so pasta stirred into a favourite purée is a good way to introduce more texture.

Also offer finger foods alongside his meals (see page 61). Start with soft foods, such as steamed carrots and broccoli or avocado, and move on to slightly harder foods, such as toast fingers and well-cooked pasta shapes, before he's comfortable with chewing, when you can introduce cubes of soft cheese, dried apricots, and chunks of meat, for example. See more advice on page 61.

Once your toddler starts to experiment a little and becomes more comfortable with lumps, it's a good idea to encourage him to stir "lumpy" ingredients into his foods, such as raisins into cereal, or to dip finger foods into purées. Over time, all will be well.

Q What are the best finger foods for this age group?

A Incorporating as many different food groups as you can will make a big difference to the number of nutrients your toddler gets. Raw vegetables, such as carrot sticks, cucumber, or strips of red pepper, are often more popular than cooked. Try some more unusual vegetables, too. Crunchy sugar snap peas are delicious – serve them with hummus. Berries, grapes, mango, apple, and banana are all healthy snacks. You can also make fresh fruit ice lollies by blending fruits together with fruit juice or yogurt and freezing in mini ice-lolly moulds – chewing on something cold will also help relieve your toddler's sore gums. For wholesome carbohydrates, choose breadsticks, wholemeal toast fingers, finger sandwiches, flapjacks, rice cakes, healthy breakfast cereals, and well-cooked pasta. As long as there is no risk of choking, anything goes!

★ finger food dips

Make a dip for dipping vegetable batons by blending together 125g (4½oz) cottage cheese, 2 tbsp mayonnaise, a heaped tbsp tomato ketchup, and a squeeze of lemon juice. For a more fruity dip, blend together a little cottage cheese with some sugar, a few drops of vanilla, and some apricot purée.

PREPARATION TIME 15 MINUTES | COOKING TIME 4–6 MINUTES | MAKES 6–8 CHILD PORTIONS

fish goujons

Toddlers can be **notoriously faddy** about fish, but most like these **baby-sized fish fingers** made with tender white fish. While they're perfect for little hands, **the whole family** will enjoy them too.

45g (1½oz) dried breadcrumbs

30g (1oz) Parmesan cheese, grated

¼ tsp paprika (optional)

Freshly ground black pepper

1 egg

1 tsp water

2 tbsp plain flour

225g (8oz) fresh white fish fillet, such as cod or sole, cut into little finger-sized strips (if you are planning to freeze the goujons, be sure the fish has not previously been frozen)

3–4 tbsp sunflower oil, for frying

1 Mix together the breadcrumbs, Parmesan, and paprika (if using) and season with pepper. Spread the crumb mixture out on a large plate.

2 Beat the egg in a bowl with the water. Spread the flour out on another large plate.

3 Coat the fish pieces in the flour, then dip in the egg and coat in the breadcrumbs. If planning to freeze, lay the coated fish goujons on a baking sheet lined with baking parchment. If cooking immediately, put them on a plate.

4 Heat the oil in a large frying pan over a moderate heat. Fry the fish goujons for 2–3 minutes on each side until they are golden and the fish is just cooked through. Drain on kitchen paper. Check the temperature before serving.

5 To freeze (uncooked), cover the baking sheet with cling film and freeze for 2–3 hours until the fish is firm. Transfer to a sealable plastic bag or box and store in the freezer. Cook from frozen, adding about 30 seconds per side extra cooking time.

always on the go

Your toddler will be **raring to go**, and keen to try many new experiences. It isn't always easy to keep up with an energetic toddler, and to ensure he's getting all the nutrients he needs. But **it's not as hard as you may think** to keep things going on the run, whether he's in childcare, at nursery school, or dining with friends.

Q How can I be sure my child gets a balanced diet when she is at nursery?

A It can be difficult to work out what your little one is eating at nursery, unless you send her with a packed lunch. Most nurseries will happily provide details of the weekly menu plan, and most will contain a good balance of healthy foods. Several studies show that young children can be more adventurous when eating with friends, so she may end up trying and eating a wider variety of foods than she would at home. If she eats all three meals at nursery, talk to nursery staff to see what she is eating regularly, and where the shortfalls might be. If it appears that she isn't eating well at nursery, consider sending in a packed lunch, and ask that anything she doesn't eat be returned to you so that you can see what is actually going in!

Q Can you give me some ideas for a fun but nutritious packed lunch?

A One of the easiest ways to make sandwiches more interesting is to use different types of bread. Mini bagels and wraps (flour tortillas) are also good for sandwiches. I like to roll slices of bread with a rolling pin so that it is thinner for sandwiches. You can then use cutters to cut the sandwiches into fun shapes. There are plenty of sandwich filling ideas on pages 97 and 191. If your child doesn't eat sandwiches you could try deconstructing the sandwich and making fillings, such as cream cheese and peanut butter, into dips (stir in a little milk to soften the consistency). Give strips of ham and cheese plus mini rice cakes, unsalted crackers, or cold cooked pasta to eat with the dips.

On page 144 I have suggested a range of healthy lunchbox ideas. As it is often a rush to get yourself and your child out of the house in the morning, each of these can be assembled in less than 10 minutes.

To help keep lunches cool invest in an insulated lunchbox or bag and cold pack that can be frozen every night. Add a juice box each day as fruit juice counts as one of the five-a-day fruit and vegetable requirements. Snack-sized boxes of raisins are also a good addition.

★ did you know ...

that fussy eaters are almost always willing to try new things if their friends are doing so, so why not invite a friend for tea and add a few different goodies to the menu? Try meeting up with friends and their toddlers at different venues, such as a restaurant or park, to see if this sparks an interest in something your toddler may not have tried before. Picnics with other toddler friends can provide a wonderful opportunity for your little one to try a variety of different finger foods.

Q Is it OK to rely on jars occasionally?

A There is no reason why the occasional jar of toddler or baby food can't be used for the sake of convenience. Problems begin when you over-rely on them, or use them exclusively. In this case, babies and toddlers become used to the bland flavours and the over-processed texture, making the transition to family food more difficult.

Q Why are jarred foods so appealing to babies and toddlers?

A First of all, babies who have been weaned on to homemade baby foods don't seem to have the same interest in jarred foods – probably because they seem tasteless in comparison to their normal fare. However, little ones whose first tastes have come from jars do find them appealing because they are completely unchallenging. The flavours are often bland, they lack the vibrant colours of freshly made fruit and vegetables, and there tends to be little texture. Furthermore, while baby foods for very small babies do not usually contain salt or sugar, jarred foods for toddlers may contain both, as well as other ingredients, such as flavourings, which obviously makes them more attractive.

Q I have very little time to cook in the evenings but don't want to rely on ready meals. Can you suggest nutritious recipes I can make in a hurry?

A Homemade burgers are easy to prepare (see page 185). It's a good idea to make a batch of these and freeze them on a tray lined with clingfilm. Once frozen, wrap each one in clingfilm and store in freezer bags or plastic boxes so that it is easy to take out as many as you need. Grilled chicken yakitori (page 150) is also a quick, delicious meal for the whole family. Try the Cheese and ham pit-zas, on the following page – these take just 15 minutes, so are the ultimate fast food. Try the very quick-to-make Chicken quesadillas (see page 28), too, which the whole family can enjoy. It's a fantastic idea to make a large batch of Hidden-vegetable tomato sauce (see page 183), as this is so versatile; it can be used with all manner of pasta dishes and as a pizza topping too.

PREPARATION TIME 5 MINUTES | COOKING TIME 10 MINUTES | MAKES 1 CHILD PORTION

cheese and ham pit-zas

Pittas make a **nice crisp base for pizzas** – or pit-zas! Try my tomato sauce on page 183 or use a good-quality store-bought sauce. If you only have large pittas, **then warm and split one** as described in the recipe, and just use one half. Another good base for a pizza is a **split toasted muffin.** For a vegetarian version, leave out the ham.

1 small, round pitta bread (about 8cm/3in diameter)

2 tbsp tomato sauce

30g (1oz) mozzarella or Cheddar cheese, grated

½ thin slice of ham, cut into thin strips

1 tsp sliced black olives (optional)

2–3 fresh basil leaves, to garnish (optional)

1 Preheat the oven to 200°C (180°C fan), gas 6.

2 Warm the pitta bread in a microwave for about 10 seconds, then carefully split in half to give two thin rounds. Place the pitta halves on a baking sheet, crumb side up. Spread tomato sauce over the rounds and scatter on the cheese, ham, and olives, if using.

3 Bake for 9–10 minutes until the cheese has melted and the pitta is crisp. Cool slightly before cutting each pit-za into four. Scatter a little torn basil on top to garnish, if you like.

★ **Variations:** Toast the pitta halves under the grill, then add the toppings and continue cooking under the grill until the cheese melts. For hungry toddlers or older children, use a whole mini pitta.

packed lunch ideas

If your child is in a nursery or daycare facility that requires a packed lunch, or **you're out and about**, it can be difficult to come up with ideas. Here are some great lunches that cover all the **requirements for a balanced meal**.

lunchbox 1

- Cheese or ham sandwiches (cut into fun shapes) or mini bagels
- Carrot and cucumber sticks
- Pitta bread fingers with hummus
- Yogurt
- Apple slices and halved grapes
- Smoothie or 100 per cent juice

lunchbox 2

- Cheese slices cut into shapes plus strips of ham packed into pots
- Mini rice cakes or unsalted crackers (lightly butter them first, if you like)
- Blueberries or quartered grapes
- Oat and raisin cookie (or yogurt/ fromage frais)

lunchbox 3

- Tuna mini sub – fill a split hot dog bun with 30g (1oz) drained canned tuna, 2 tsp Greek yogurt, ½ tsp tomato ketchup, 2–3 drops of lemon juice, and ¼ tsp sweet chilli sauce (optional)
- Carrot sticks
- Cottage cheese and pineapple pot (or yogurt)

lunchbox 4

- Cream cheese and fruit wrap – spread 1–2 tbsp cream cheese over a flour tortilla and scatter on small pieces of dried apricots or add a thin layer of good-quality fruit spread. Roll up and cut into 3–4 pieces.
- Cucumber sticks
- Mini muffin (or yogurt/fromage frais)

lunchbox 5

- Peanut butter on mini bagel
- Creamy potato salad with chopped ham or chicken
- Apple slices

lunchbox 6

- Cheese sandwich on wholegrain bread
- Melon and strawberry salad (cut into bite-sized pieces)
- Yogurt

lunchbox 7

- Pasta salad with chicken, lightly cooked broccoli, and sweetcorn, and a dressing made with 1½ tbsp light olive oil and ½ tbsp each of honey, soy sauce, and lemon juice
- Probiotic yogurt drink
- Mini pack of dried fruit
- Cereal bar or fruity muffin

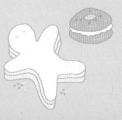

flavours from around the world

Family meals offer **a great opportunity** to encourage your toddler to try new foods, and to **experiment with new tastes.** Too many people assume that babies and toddlers want bland, tasteless meals, when, in fact, most of them **love to try new flavours,** and **have sensitive palates** right from the word go.

Q **My toddler's food seems a little bland. Do you have any ideas to help me spice it up?**

A The idea that you can't add herbs and spices to a toddler's food is long out of date. It's absolutely fine to experiment with different flavours and textures, to make your toddler's diet not only more exciting, but to introduce her to a more varied diet.

Some little ones might find hot spices difficult to manage, but focusing on more fragrant options, such as coriander, lemongrass, thyme, cardamom, cinnamon, dill, and oregano are all good options. Consider adding some fruit juice, such as lime, orange, apricot, or even grape, for flavour, or seasoning with a little ground black pepper, some wine (as long as it's cooked at a high enough temperature to evaporate the alcohol), a little mild curry paste, coconut milk, sweet chilli sauce, soy sauce, or garlic. Consider offering some unusual combinations, such as adding fruit to meat or vegetables to puddings; not only will you be bumping up her nutrient intake, but you will be adding flavour, texture, and fibre to old favourites. The greater the range of flavours to which your toddler is introduced in the early years, the more expansive her palate will be.

Q **How can I encourage my toddler to try new tastes?**

A The great thing about hungry toddlers is that they'll normally eat what's put in front of them. So when your little one is tired out from time at the park, nursery school, or a play date, have a bowl ready, full of whatever healthy, new tastes you want your child to try. She'll tuck in before she has a chance to ask for anything else! See the tips for making food extra-tasty (left and overleaf).

★ **dining out**

Eating out with your toddler can be fun, but it's a good idea to make sure you arrive at the restaurant well before her usual dinner time, and to avoid busy periods, which can result in delays. Bring along a selection of finger foods and some distractions, such as crayons, to keep her busy while she waits, and ask for her food to arrive as soon as it's ready.

Q What are some good ways to introduce new spices and other tastes?

A If your toddler is used to plain purées and bland meals, she may be a little more reluctant to try new tastes. Little ones also have an amazing ability to spot anything that looks different, such as a sprig of dill, or a sprinkling of chopped basil, and may pick out the offending items. At the outset, try using herbs and other spices to flavour food while cooking, and then strain them out before serving. Another option is to purée them into a sauce, so they are not immediately obvious. Once your toddler is accustomed to the taste, you can leave in increasingly larger bits of seasoning, until they are accepted. I find that pesto is popular with little ones; see the recipe opposite.

There are many ways to make meals flavourful, and encouraging an appreciation of different tastes will help your toddler to develop a healthy approach to food in general.

Q My toddler wants to eat the same food as the rest of the family. Which family meals are appropriate?

A Good choices include pasta dishes, such as spaghetti bolognese, lasagne (see pages 148–149), and macaroni cheese. Consider trying chicken satays with rice, tiny beef burgers (see page 185), fish cakes with potato wedges, and a fish pie with a cheese sauce. Simply make sure that salt is kept to a minimum, and everything is cut small and cooked well for your toddler to manage without choking.

Q Are restaurant meals appropriate for my one-year-old?

A Introducing your toddler to different tastes at restaurants is an excellent way to encourage both an appreciation of food, and a wider diet. Every different culture uses unique herbs, spices, and other flavourings and, in reality, none is inappropriate for little ones. While we might baulk at offering a toddler a spicy Indian meal, children around the world are brought up on similar fare with no ill-effects. I would, however, avoid foods that have high levels of fat, sugar, or salt, are deep-fried or raw, or contain MSG (an additive).

★ did you know ...

that children love to try food from different cultures? Take your child out and let her try delicious stir-fries, grilled chicken satays with peanut sauce, mild curries, thin-crust vegetable-topped pizzas, spaghetti bolognese, lean chicken kebabs, grilled fish and breaded fish balls. A word of warning, though: if your child suffers from food allergies, it is often difficult to avoid cross-contamination in some restaurants, so when in doubt, steer clear.

PREPARATION TIME 10 MINUTES | COOKING TIME 13–17 MINUTES | SERVES A FAMILY OF 4–5

pesto pasta with chicken and cherry tomatoes

Children seem to love pesto, even those who shy away from green foods! **Making your own is easy** and it **keeps very well**, although you can use 100g (3½oz) pesto from a jar instead. Vegetarians can replace the chicken **with cubed fresh mozzarella**.

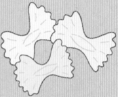

300g (10oz) pasta, such as farfalle, fusilli, or spaghetti

30g (1oz) bunch of fresh basil, stems discarded

½ garlic clove

30g (1oz) pine nuts, lightly toasted

6 tbsp olive oil, plus 1 tsp extra

30g (1oz) Parmesan cheese, grated, plus extra to serve

Salt and freshly ground black pepper

1–2 tbsp boiling water

115g (4oz) cherry tomatoes, halved

175g (6oz) cooked chicken, shredded

1 Cook the pasta in boiling water according to the packet instructions. Meanwhile, make the pesto. Put the basil leaves in a food processor with the garlic. Process to a purée, then add the pine nuts and process until the nuts are finely chopped, stopping and scraping down the sides of the processor bowl as necessary. Keep the motor running and trickle 6 tbsp of the olive oil into the processor. When all the oil is mixed in, add the Parmesan and salt and pepper to taste, and pulse three or four times to combine. Add just enough boiling water to thin slightly.

2 Drain the pasta and set aside. Put the extra 1 tsp oil in the empty pasta pan and add the tomatoes. Fry them gently for 2–3 minutes until just softening. Add the pesto and chicken and heat through for 1–2 minutes (the chicken must be piping hot). Add the cooked, drained pasta and toss everything together. Spoon on to serving plates and serve with extra Parmesan.

PREPARATION TIME 1 HOUR | COOKING TIME 35–40 MINUTES | SERVES A FAMILY OF 4–5

lasagne al forno

Nothing is more of **a crowd-pleaser** than a big dish of baked lasagne – at any age and any time of year! Mixing the meat and cheese sauces may sound odd, but **it makes the sauce taste richer**.

1 tbsp olive oil, plus extra to grease

1 red onion, chopped

1 carrot, peeled and grated

55g (2oz) chestnut mushrooms, chopped

1 garlic clove, crushed

400g (14oz) can chopped tomatoes

4 tbsp tomato purée

2 tbsp tomato ketchup

450g (1lb) lean minced beef

150ml (5fl oz) beef stock

1 tsp soft light brown sugar

¼ tsp dried oregano

9 sheets no-precook lasagne

85g (3oz) mozzarella cheese, grated

30g (1oz) grated Parmesan cheese

Cheese sauce

4 tbsp cornflour

600ml (1 pint) milk

115g (4oz) mascarpone

Freshly grated nutmeg

1 Heat the oil in a large, deep frying pan and cook the vegetables gently until soft and lightly browned. Add the garlic and cook for 1 minute. Transfer the vegetables to a blender and add the tomatoes, tomato purée, and ketchup. Blend until smooth. Set aside.

2 Brown the mince in the pan, then add the tomato mixture, beef stock, sugar, and oregano. Simmer for about 30 minutes or until thick. Season to taste.

3 Make the cheese sauce by mixing the cornflour in a saucepan with a little of the milk until smooth. Whisk in the remaining milk. Bring to the boil and cook, whisking, for 1 minute or until thick. Remove from the heat and stir in the mascarpone. Season to taste with nutmeg, salt, and pepper.

4 Lightly oil a large rectangular ovenproof dish (about 28 x 18cm/11 x 7in). Mix half of the cheese sauce into the meat sauce. Spread 2 tbsp of the remaining cheese sauce over the bottom of the dish, then put on a layer of three lasagne sheets. Spoon over half of the meat mixture, then add another layer of pasta. Spoon over the remaining meat mixture and top with a final layer of pasta. Cover with the remaining cheese sauce and scatter the grated cheeses over the surface.

5 Preheat the oven to 190°C (170°C fan), gas 5. Bake
the lasagne for 35–40 minutes until golden brown
on top and cooked through. Test by inserting a knife
down through the centre; you should feel no
resistance. Leave to stand for 10 minutes before
cutting and serving.

6 The unbaked lasagne can be kept in the fridge,
covered, until needed (up to 24 hours ahead). It can
also be frozen, wrapped well in foil; thaw in the fridge
for 24 hours. To bake a chilled or thawed lasagne,
preheat the oven to 180°C (160°C fan), gas 4. Bake
for 40 minutes, then increase the oven to 200°C
(180°C fan), gas 6 and bake for a further 10 minutes
or until golden brown on top and piping hot. Leave
to stand for 10 minutes before cutting and serving.

PREPARATION TIME 10 MINUTES | COOKING TIME 15 MINUTES | SERVES A FAMILY OF 4–5

grilled chicken yakitori

I find that grilled skewers of **chicken thigh** are more tender and moist than chicken breast, and this yakitori glaze is delicious. **These skewers** would also be **great cooked on a barbecue.**

4 fairly large skinless, boneless chicken thighs

4 spring onions

4 small bamboo skewers, soaked in water for at least 20 minutes

2–3 tbsp sunflower oil

Yakitori glaze

3 tbsp soy sauce

3 tbsp mirin (sweet Japanese rice wine)

3 tbsp clear honey

2 tsp rice vinegar

1 tsp grated fresh root ginger

1 small garlic clove, crushed

1 To make the glaze, combine all the ingredients in a small saucepan and bring to the boil. Reduce the heat to moderate and simmer, stirring occasionally, for about 5 minutes or until reduced to a fairly thick and syrupy glaze.

2 While the glaze cooks, trim away the excess fat from the chicken thighs. Cut each thigh into three pieces – they'll be about 2cm (¾in) wide. Cut each spring onion into three pieces.

3 Preheat the grill and line the grill rack with foil. Open out the pieces of chicken and thread concertina-fashion on to the soaked skewers, alternating with the spring onions. You should have three pieces of each on a skewer. Place on the foil and brush all over with oil.

4 Grill for about 5 minutes on each side, then turn the skewers and brush with half the glaze. Grill for 3 minutes, then turn over again and brush with the remaining glaze. Grill for a final 2–3 minutes or until the chicken is cooked through.

5 Remove the chicken from the skewers and serve, with the cooking juices spooned over if you like.

fussy eaters

Don't be surprised if your **newly independent toddler** stamps his foot and demands his own way. Fussy eating is a hallmark of the toddler years; **it's best to relax** and let it run its course. Persevere and continue to **offer new foods** confidently and positively.

Q **If my toddler flatly refuses a food over and over again, should I give up?**

A Many toddlers are averse to trying new foods, but the good news is that research consistently shows that with perseverance, most will accept them eventually. The trick is to present the food in an enthusiastic manner, so that your toddler associates new tastes with a positive experience, and to continue offering it – in different guises, if necessary – until it becomes "familiar". If the same courgettes keep appearing on her plate week after week, she'll soon lose interest in resisting them, and simply get on with the job of eating.

If your toddler shows a violent dislike to a certain food, gags or vomits when eating it, and refuses it repeatedly, you may want to discuss this with a doctor. You can try to leave that food off the menu for a month or so and then try again. Or, you can change the format of how you serve that particular food to your little one. If she won't try a scrambled egg, for example, then offer some French toast instead. If the response is the same, don't push it. It may be a temporary aversion, or something more long-term, and you'll do no good by forcing her to eat something she genuinely doesn't like.

Q **My child only likes sweet foods, and won't eat anything savoury. What should I do?**

A There is no doubt that the majority of toddlers prefer sweet tastes, but research indicates that most food and flavour preferences are "learned" rather than "instinctive". In a nutshell, this means that early experiences with food are important in developing a liking for different tastes. So, don't give up! Start by blending together sweet and savoury – pork with apple purée, for example, or chicken tagine with sweet potato and dried apricots. Choose some naturally sweet savoury foods, such as sweet potato, squash, or even red peppers, whose bright colours may also convince him that they are sweeter than they are. Gradually decrease the "sweet" element of the dishes, until he is eating savoury foods. Ultimately, however, if you continue to serve just savoury foods, he will develop a taste for them.

Q My toddler will only eat fruit, and no vegetables. How can I encourage better eating habits?

A Fruit is undoubtedly sweeter and more instantly satisfying than the average vegetable, but it doesn't supply the full range of vitamins and, in particular, minerals that your child needs. Try mixing fruit with vegetables – couscous with sultanas, apricots, sautéed peppers, and onions is a good start. As long as the "fruity" taste is overwhelming, she'll probably give it a go. Also use both fruit and vegetable juices when cooking savoury dishes. Try to use vegetables and fruit together too – a chicken dish with fresh pineapple and dried apricots goes well with water chestnuts and steamed spinach.

⭐ breakfast fare

Make breakfast time fun. If your toddler is resistant, offer a range of healthy options, and ask him to choose from them. A little platter with some fruit, a few squares of toast with peanut butter, a boiled egg with soldiers, and a handful of breakfast cereal (see recipe, right) may tempt him. If necessary, offer a favourite sandwich and some cubes of fruit, or leftover pasta shapes and chicken. Once he becomes accustomed to breakfast, you can revert to more standard fare.

Q How can I stop mealtimes becoming a battleground?

A Most toddlers have periods of faddy eating. One reason is that they are asserting their independence and like to have a say in what they do. This can make mealtimes tense for everyone. The most important thing you can do is to try not to make a fuss. If your toddler realizes that you are upset or angry when he doesn't eat, he's gained an emotional advantage, which he can play whenever he chooses. If you don't react, he'll likely choose a new battle. Continue offering the food you want him to eat, and silently removing the plate when he has eaten (or not eaten) what he wishes. When he realizes that he isn't going to get a reaction by resisting certain foods, he'll likely eat them. It's also a good idea to offer your child choices (see page 180).

Q My toddler is a faddy eater. Should I offer supplements?

A While a healthy, varied diet will provide your toddler with the vitamins and minerals she needs for good health, faddy eating does mean that her diet is limited. For example, a fussy toddler who refuses to eat fruit and vegetables will be missing vitamins and minerals that are essential for her growth and development, as well as her immunity to infections. If she doesn't eat meat, she may well be low in iron, which will affect her concentration and energy levels, among other things (see page 201). The Department of Health recommends vitamin supplements for all under-twos, which can help to supply what's missing, and ease your mind, too. They can never take the place of a healthy diet, but they're a good stopgap when kids resist our attempts to serve healthy meals. Drop form is best for under-twos.

PREPARATION TIME 5 MINUTES | COOKING TIME 25 MINUTES | MAKES ABOUT 8 CHILD PORTIONS

honey, oat, and raisin crisp

Oats make a good breakfast cereal as they contain **slow-burn carbohydrates** that help to keep blood sugar levels on an even keel until snack time. Serve this with **milk and delicious fresh berries** to tempt even the fussiest little eater.

175g (6oz) rolled oats

15g (½oz) desiccated coconut

Pinch of salt

55g (2oz) soft light brown sugar

2 tbsp sunflower oil, plus a little extra
  for greasing

2 tbsp clear honey

1 tsp vanilla extract

55g (2oz) raisins

30g (1oz) sunflower seeds (optional)

To serve

Milk and fresh berries

1 Preheat the oven to 160°C (140°C fan), gas 3.

2 Put the oats in a large bowl and stir in the coconut, salt, and sugar. Whisk together the oil, honey, and vanilla extract and pour over the oats. Stir until the oats are evenly coated, then spread out in a lightly oiled baking tray.

3 Bake for about 25 minutes or until golden and crisp, stirring several times. Watch carefully towards the end of the cooking time to make sure the oats don't burn. Cool on the baking tray, then mix in the raisins and sunflower seeds, if using. Store in an airtight container.

4 Serve each portion (about 2 tbsp, depending on appetite) with cold milk and topped with berries.

weighty issues

As long as your toddler is **a confident eater**, with a varied diet full of fresh nutritious food, she'll continue to grow at the right rate for her. It's also **normal for babies** to gain a little extra weight before a **growth spurt** or to appear thinner **following a period of growth** or an illness – all is fine so long as she remains healthy and eats well.

Q **How can I tell if my toddler is overweight?**

A The very best way to assess your toddler's weight is to use the growth charts provided by your doctor or health visitor when your child is born. Ideally, she will remain on roughly the same centile line through childhood (although there can be blips during periods of intensive growth). If she suddenly leaps up two centile lines, there may be cause for concern.

Doctors will soon be offering BMI charts as well. BMI stands for body mass index, which is calculated using height and weight to estimate how much body fat someone has. It helps determine how appropriate a child's weight is for a certain height and age. All charts are there for guidance, and it's important to use common sense as well when assessing weight. If your child has no obvious rolls of fat, and fits the clothing sizes appropriate for her age, chances are that all is well.

Q **My toddler seems very thin even though he has a healthy diet. Could he be underweight?**

A Some children are naturally slim and slight. If your child is healthy, has plenty of energy, and is growing normally, there should be no cause for concern. Continue to plot his weight on his growth chart, and as long as he is sitting along his ususal centile, there is little to worry about. If he does appear to be falling below what is normal for him, then visit your doctor to investigate why.

Q **Is it OK to serve my child full-fat milk?**

A Absolutely yes, and this is to be encouraged. Unless your child is overweight, and your doctor advises against it, full-fat milk and other dairy products should be served to anyone under the age of two or three. This is because there are plenty of fat-soluble vitamins in milk, such as vitamin D, which children need for the development of healthy bones. Also, fat is very important for toddlers as it is required for brain development (see right). Milk is a nutritionally dense food, and provides your toddler with the calories she needs to keep going and growing.

Q How much fat does my toddler need, and does it matter what type?

A Fat is one of the six groups of nutrients that are essential for growth and development (the others are protein, water, vitamins, carbohydrate, and minerals). During early childhood, fat is extremely important as little ones grow and develop quickly. Fat is an important source of energy, and it also carries the fat-soluble vitamins A, D, E, and K, which are essential for health. Fat is also the only source of essential fatty acids (EFAs), which are implicated in a whole host of health benefits, in particular, overall brain development. They have also been shown to play a role in preventing heart disease in later life.

Ensure that your child gets plenty of healthy fats, which include those found in lean meats, poultry, fish, eggs, dairy produce, nuts, and seeds. Avocados are also a great source of healthy fats, in particular EFAs. Offer some fat at every meal in one of these forms.

It is very important to avoid giving your little one transfats, which are used in a wide number of processed foods and baked goods. If you see the word "hydrogenated" on any food label, it contains transfats, so you'll need to give it a miss.

Q Is it OK to serve creamy, fatty foods to encourage my toddler to put on some weight?

A If your child is underweight, fatty foods can provide her with the calories she needs. However, this doesn't mean serving up plates of unhealthy food. The key is to offer nutrient-dense, healthy foods instead of fatty junk foods, containing transfats (see left). Add eggs and full-fat dairy products to your child's diet, as well as more seeds and nuts. Stir a little cream and grated cheese into her scrambled eggs, or make some tempting sauces to add to her pasta or vegetables. Use olive oil and butter in cooking, and offer full-fat yogurt or fromage frais with snacks.

It's important, however, to find a balance. Ensure your child is eating plenty of other healthy foods alongside. While creamy, fatty foods can have a pretty quick impact on weight, they can also be habit-forming, and your child may develop eating habits that can be hard to shift later on.

★ did you know ...

that snacks are important for toddlers for a number of reasons? The first is that toddlers' tummies are not big enough to eat sufficient food during a meal to keep them going until the next one. What's more, it takes a very focused toddler to sit down and eat an entire meal without losing concentration, so even the healthiest meals may go largely untouched. Well-timed snacks can help to balance out an uneven diet, and provide energy to keep your child healthy and happy.

Q Do portion sizes matter at this age?

A It helps to know that a serving of fruit and vegetables is roughly what your child can hold in his hand. Also, protein, like chicken or beef, should be the size of your child's palm, and fish should be the size of his hand. So, two peas and a single grape is unlikely to make the grade, and one bite of chicken will not form a portion, either. The best advice is to tot up your child's overall intake across a day, to work out roughly how many servings of each food group your child has eaten. For example, he may eat only one bite of chicken at dinner time, but if he's had two or three other forms of protein throughout the day, that's fine!

★ healthy snacks

These might include the following:

- Natural yogurt (not low-fat) mixed with fruit purée or honey
- Yogurt-coated rice cakes
- Split toasted English muffins topped with sliced tomatoes and grated cheese, and grilled for two minutes
- Fruity flapjack (see opposite page)
- Cubes of fruit and raisins
- Nut butters on wholegrain toast
- Mini sandwiches, for example, tuna mixed with tomato ketchup and a little mayonnaise; cream cheese and low-sugar jam; peanut butter, etc.

Q My toddler seems to graze rather than eat proper meals. Should I cut out snacks?

A The problem is that constant snacking can become a habit, leaving little ones with no appetite for their main meals. The best advice is to choose a time – mid-morning, mid-afternoon, and perhaps just before bed – for snacks. Don't offer anything else around these snack times, but do make sure that the snacks you choose are healthy (see below), as they constitute an important part of your child's overall diet. Offer plenty of water throughout the day, too, because thirst is often mistaken for hunger in little ones. Some toddlers are "little and often" eaters, and can't seem to manage an entire meal in a sitting. In this case, as long as you consider each snack a small meal, and make sure each is balanced, it's fine to go with it until he's able to eat a little more at one sitting.

Q How many snacks should my toddler be eating?

A One snack between each meal, and perhaps one before bed, should be adequate for most toddlers. Some don't manage much in a sitting, in which case you could, for example, offer a few squares of toast an hour or so after breakfast, and some cubed fruit or raisins a little later. As long as you avoid offering a snack at least an hour before mealtime, your toddler should be hungry enough to eat well. Let your child's hunger dictate things to some extent. If she is a healthy weight, very active, and eating a reasonable amount at mealtimes, she may need more fuel between stops. The trick is to choose well, with healthy, nutritious snacks that will enhance rather than detract from her overall diet.

PREPARATION TIME 10 MINUTES | COOKING TIME 20 MINUTES | MAKES 16 BARS OR 20 SQUARES

fruity flapjacks

Active children need to have **regular snacks**, particularly toddlers who can be **so busy with life** in general that it is often difficult to get them to stop for regular meals. The oats in these flapjacks will provide **long-lasting energy**. For a plain flapjack, leave out the raisins and sultanas.

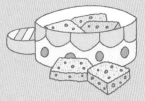

100g (3½oz) butter

115g (4oz) soft light brown sugar

2 tbsp golden syrup

225g (8oz) rolled oats

30g (1oz) raisins

30g (1oz) sultanas

30g (1oz) dried cranberries (optional)

¼ tsp salt

1 egg, beaten

1 tsp vanilla extract

1 Preheat the oven to 180°C (160°C fan), gas 4. Line an 28 x 18cm (11 x 7in) shallow baking tin with baking parchment; cut the paper so it is large enough to extend above the sides of the tin.

2 Put the butter, sugar, and golden syrup in a saucepan and heat gently, stirring occasionally, until the butter and sugar have melted. Set aside to cool slightly.

3 Combine the oats, fruits, and salt in a large bowl. Add the egg, vanilla extract, and cooled butter mixture and mix together well. Spoon into the prepared tin and spread out evenly. Press down firmly with a potato masher or the back of the spoon (or your fingers). Bake for about 20 minutes or until golden brown and firm to the touch.

4 Leave to cool in the tin, then lift out using the baking parchment. Cut into bars or squares and store in an airtight container.

a sweet tooth?

Some little ones seem to be born with a sweet tooth, no matter **how scrupulously savoury** their weaning menu has been! Sweets and treats do have a place in your toddler's healthy, balanced diet, but it's important to **get the balance right**.

Q **My toddler has a sweet tooth. How can I satisfy her with healthier alternatives?**

A Many toddlers instinctively prefer sweet foods to savoury alternatives, and if they become used to foods that contain added sugar, they'll find the natural sweetness of healthy options, such as fruit, bland and boring.

If you have added sugar to your toddler's food in the past, cut down rather than remove it completely. If she's used to sweetness, she may resist anything without sugar. Try sweetening your child's food with fruit juice or fruit purée instead. While this is still sugar in another form, it is healthier because unlike refined sugar it contains vitamins and minerals. Similarly, maple syrup, molasses, and honey offer nutrients while they sweeten, making them a much healthier option. Work towards providing plenty of fresh, natural foods that are sweet in their own right, and present less risk of tooth decay and health problems.

Q **My toddler seems to be quite hyperactive after eating anything sweet. What can I offer instead?**

A Many children are sensitive to sugar, and get a burst of uncontrollable energy after eating anything sweet, particularly if it contains refined white sugar. The down side is that soon after they have eaten it, they "crash" as their blood sugar levels fall, and can become tearful, tired, and grumpy. However, sweet does not necessarily mean unhealthy. Fresh fruit is high in naturally occurring sugars, but because of the fibre content of the fruit, it tends to be digested more slowly than other sugary foods, which prevents that surge of wild energy. Similarly, dried fruit is sweet, but also healthy.

Adding a little protein alongside (a yogurt dip for fruit, for example, or a few chunks of cheese, or even a little ham) can slow down the transit of sweeter foods, and prevent the hyperactive effect. Try to get your toddler used to eating a better balance of savoury and sweet. Healthy never has to mean boring, and if you keep on presenting some interesting and delicious meals, your toddler will quickly forget all about the sweets that were once a bigger part of his diet.

Q Are there any sweets that are appropriate for this age group?

A Children under the age of two don't need sweets as such, and they are unlikely to object to not being given them. That doesn't mean that they can't have sweet "treats" from time to time, such as delicious fruit tarts or puddings (see Blueberry-lime cheesecakes on page 161), or even jellies , fresh fruit ice lollies (see page 116) and high fruit spreads. The longer you can resist giving in to packaged sweets, the better the chance that your toddler will develop good eating habits, and a healthy diet. One exception is a little good-quality chocolate (if your child likes it). It may do nothing for your child's teeth, but it does have some health benefits that most other sweets do not.

Q Are there any "healthy" foods that might damage my toddler's teeth?

A Many healthy foods contain high levels of natural sugar, such as lactose (in milk) and fructose (in fruit). Milk, fruit juice, fruit, and dried fruit can all cause problems with teeth if they are consumed between meals. Dried fruit in particular is quite sticky, and can stay on the teeth for longer periods of time, creating the conditions that cause decay, and fruit juice can be very damaging. For this reason, it's a good idea to offer these foods with meals, rather than as snacks, and offer a cube of cheese or a few spoonfuls of yogurt alongside, as these serve to neutralize the acid that can lead to problems. Offer sweet snacks such as raisins in a short time space, thereby limiting the damage they might cause if your child spends the afternoon grazing on them. If your toddler is still on a night-time bottle, don't allow him to go to bed with it.

Q Should I brush my toddler's teeth after sweet snacks?

A Interestingly, it's not a good idea to brush teeth immediately after sweet snacks, as the acid they contain damages the enamel, and brushing immediately can cause bits of enamel to be brushed away. Dentists recommend waiting at least an hour before brushing teeth after eating. This allows your toddler's saliva to get to work. Saliva is saturated with calcium and phosphate, which promotes the remineralization of teeth. It also neutralizes the acids produced by bacteria and acts as a reservoir for fluoride, which also works to ensure that teeth are remineralized, and bacterial acid is inhibited. It is, however, a good idea to give your little one some water to "rinse" her mouth after eating.

★ ditch the fizz

A typical 330ml (12fl oz) can of fizzy drink contains about 5 teaspoons of sugar. Diet drinks aren't much better because, like most fizzy drinks, they contain acids that have been linked to drawing the calcium from our bones. The acids in fruit juices and smoothies are also bad for children's teeth. It's best to give fruit juice and smoothies at mealtimes and only give water between meals.

PREPARATION TIME 15 MINUTES | MAKES 4

blueberry-lime cheesecakes

This dessert is **ideal for little ones** as it makes small, individual cheesecakes. They are **fun to make with your child** – he can help crush the biscuits, mix the filling, and put the fruit on top. A ginger **biscuit base and raspberries** are nice alternatives.

85g (3oz) digestive biscuits

45g (1½oz) butter, melted

55g (2oz) cream cheese, at room temperature

4 tbsp Greek yogurt

Grated zest and juice of 1 lime

30g (1oz) icing sugar, sifted

100ml (3½fl oz) double cream

To serve

About 85g (3oz) blueberries

Icing sugar

1 Put the digestives in a freezer bag and crush to fine crumbs with a rolling pin. Stir the crumbs into the melted butter. Divide among four individual 7.5cm (3in) diameter loose-bottomed flan tins and press the crumbs evenly over the bottom.

2 Put the cream cheese in a bowl and beat to soften slightly. Add the yogurt, lime zest and juice, and sugar, and beat to combine. Whip the cream in a separate bowl until it makes soft peaks, then fold into the cream cheese mixture.

3 Spoon the filling into the tins over the crumb bases. Cover and chill for at least 2 hours, or overnight, to set. Or freeze the cheesecakes; when needed, thaw overnight in the fridge.

4 Remove the side from each tin, then use a palette knife to carefully lift the cheesecake from the tin bottom and place on a plate. Top each cheesecake with blueberries and dust with sifted icing sugar before serving.

your toddler's health

What your little one eats will impact on his health, and it's important to provide him with **meals that give him energy**, promote his **growth and development**, and keep his moods and his immune system on an even keel. What's more, your toddler's balanced diet will begin to develop his **taste for a healthy lifestyle**.

Q Is it true that too much sugar can make my child more susceptible to infections?

A Studies have hinted that sugar affects the immune system, which is especially apparent in sick children. It is good practice to avoid adding sugar to foods, and choosing products without added sugar, whether your child is ill or not, as this will encourage good health and reduce the risk of tooth decay (see pages 158–159).

★ healthy sweets

It's always a good idea to encourage your little ones to enjoy the natural sweetness of foods, but when you need a little something to make tart foods more palatable, go for honey (after 12 months), molasses, or maple syrup. Unlike refined sugar, these sweeteners are rich in nutrients that will encourage health rather than undermine it! Honey in particular contains enzymes that act as a natural antiseptic.

Q What foods can boost my toddler's immune system?

A Antioxidants, such as vitamins A, C, and E, beta-carotene and the minerals zinc and selenium are all important for a healthy immune system. Brightly coloured fruits and vegetables, and in particular berries, are very high in antioxidants (see opposite for more information).

Probiotics are healthy bacteria that can be taken to encourage a healthy balance of bacteria in the gut. You may be surprised to learn that your child's digestive system has such a strong role to play in her immune system, but, in fact, it represents the biggest organ of this important system. Live yogurt and very ripe bananas are good sources of probiotics, so offer these as often as you can.

EFAs (essential fatty acids) are also known to be involved in healthy immunity, so include nuts, seeds, and oily fish in your toddler's diet whenever possible. Another important nutrient is zinc, found in wholegrains, seafood, eggs, meat, and poultry, which prevents and reduces the severity of infections. Good-quality protein is also essential, and if your toddler doesn't get enough in her diet, she'll be less likely to manufacture the white blood cells required to fight off infections.

Q What are antioxidants and why does my toddler need them?

A There is a group of vitamins, minerals, and enzymes called antioxidants that help to protect the body from the formation of free radicals. Free radicals are atoms or groups of atoms that can cause damage to cells, impairing the immune system and leading to diseases such as heart disease and cancer. Antioxidants include vitamins A, C, and E, beta-carotene, and the minerals selenium and zinc, among others, and they are normally found in brightly coloured fruits and vegetables. Your toddler and every child and adult needs antioxidants to maintain good overall health and to prevent disease. You'll find good levels in carrots, squash, broccoli, sweet potatoes, tomatoes, strawberries, melon, peaches, apricots, citrus fruit, peppers, nuts, seeds, wholegrains, soya, kiwi fruit, eggs, fish, and shellfish. The more the better!

Q Is it OK if my toddler hardly eats anything when he is ill?

A Parents have a natural instinct to try to feed their children no matter what. However, the fact of the matter is that for a few days, children can survive perfectly well on a miniscule amount of food. Your child may lose a small amount of weight but babies who are otherwise healthy should make up for this when they feel better. You'll find your child may eat more than usual for a few days to make up for lost time. Continue to offer plain food to your little one, but if he's not interested, you can replace mealtimes with lots of cuddles, because that's what you need when you are feeling poorly. It's very important to ensure your child is hydrated. Offer plenty of water (see right and box on page 164).

Q Are there any foods I should avoid when my toddler has a tummy bug?

A Bland is the key word here, so avoid anything that may upset your child's tummy, such as spicy, fatty, and acidic foods (such as citrus fruit). Ripe bananas, a little plain toast, and rice are good foods to try. Peeled apples may also be useful, as they contain pectin, which helps to reduce diarrhoea, as it absorbs water and makes the stool more solid. Papaya is also high in soluble fibre, which is important for normal bowel function. It also contains enzymes that help digestion. It is a rich source of vitamin C and beta-carotene, and can help to get your toddler on the road to recovery.

It's very important to keep up fluid levels; give your toddler frequent sips of oral rehydration solution. Water is the next best thing. It's a good idea to avoid dairy products for 24 hours too.

Dehydration is a common side-effect of tummy bugs, and a serious health problem. Monitor your toddler for symptoms. Early signs include dry lips and tongue and fewer wet nappies with darker urine. More serious, later signs include clammy hands and feet and lethargy. Medical help must be sought if there is any sign of dehydration, but especially if your child is lethargic or clammy.

Q How can I tell if my toddler has food allergies?

A Symptoms differ from child to child, so the most important thing to look out for is anything unusual. With food allergies, symptoms usually appear quite quickly – often within a few minutes to a couple of hours – although some may be delayed (see pages 57–58 for more information). Common symptoms include a rash around the mouth, swollen lips, hives (urticaria, which appears as weals on the face or body), vomiting, unusual sleepiness, diarrhoea, worsening of eczema, and breathing difficulties. It's important to remember that any breathing difficulties or hoarseness should be treated as a medical emergency, and you should seek urgent medical attention. The best advice is to follow your instincts. If you think that a particular food is affecting your child's health or behaviour, see your doctor to arrange for tests (see page 58).

Q What precautions should I take when my allergic toddler goes to nursery?

A First and foremost, make sure that every member of staff is aware of your child's allergies, and knows exactly what he needs to avoid. Your doctor should provide you with an individualized "care plan" for your child's nursery, which will include the sort of symptoms to look out for, and clear instructions on what to do if they appear. The nursery should have all forms of medication to hand, and know how to use them. For example, minor symptoms can often be addressed with an antihistamine. Other children may be considered to be at particular risk of having a severe reaction and are prescribed adrenaline auto injector pens, so it is crucial that all nursery staff know how to administer adrenaline.

You will need to make sure that your toddler doesn't share anyone else's lunch, no matter how appealing it may look! If he's eating school food, you may wish to send in a "safe" packed lunch, or arrange for allergen-free meals to be served. I design the menus for a large chain of nurseries and if a child has an allergy, his plate is a different colour from the rest of the children so that the staff always know not to put certain foods on that plate.

★ did you know ...

that toddlers can easily become dehydrated when feeling ill? If your child is reluctant to drink what's on offer, try offering ice lollies made from fresh fruit juices such as pressed papaya, apple, or mango. If she turns her nose up at the oral rehydration solution – try freezing it as an ice lolly too. Sucking on ice cubes may also help. If your child has clinical signs of dehydration (see page 163) and is not improving, or is becoming lethargic or clammy, you must see a doctor.

Q **My toddler seems to flag in the afternoons; do you have any suggestions for foods that will boost her energy levels?**

A The best way to boost energy levels is to offer a healthy carbohydrate snack, which will give her a lift without causing blood sugar levels to soar and then slump. This means choosing wholegrains rather than refined carbohydrates. Adding a little protein, too, can help to ensure that digestion is slowed down and your toddler will get a sustained release of energy to keep her going. So consider some sesame breadsticks with a little hummus, oat or rice cakes with peanut butter, fresh fruit with yogurt dip, a little cheese, a few squares of a wholemeal cheese and cucumber sandwich, some pasta shapes sprinkled with grated cheese, or even a handful of breakfast cereal with some raisins and ground nuts.

Q **My toddler seems too tired to eat a proper meal in the evening. What can I offer to tempt him?**

A Why not consider offering his main meal at lunchtime, and producing a miniature platter of healthy goodies at dinner time that he can eat himself, for example, a little pasta, some cubes of cheese and raw vegetables, a few pieces of chicken or chopped egg, and some pieces of fruit. Large portions can be daunting for little ones, so consider making individual-sized portions of healthy meals, such as shepherd's pie, pasta, lasagne, vegetable bake, and fish pie, in small ramekins. It may also help to move his evening meal an hour or two earlier, and then offer him a snack or healthy pudding when the rest of the family sits down to eat (see page 208).

Q **Are there any foods that will help my toddler settle down in the evening?**

A A bigger meal is more likely to encourage her to settle down and sleep through the night. If she can't manage that, offer a nutritious snack before bed to see her through.

Protein, such as dairy produce, fish, meat, and pulses, will provide a sustained source of energy, so your little one won't wake hungry. It also tends to make us drowsy because more resources are required to digest it.

Some foods contain a substance called "tryptophan", which promotes sleep (see page 176). To encourage sleep in your little one, offer plenty of foods containing tryptophan, such as milk, eggs, meat, turkey, beans, fish, and cheese. Cheddar and gruyère are particularly rich in tryptophan.

Try to avoid offering your child anything sugary around bedtime, including whole fruit juices, which will give her a sugar hit and consequently a second wind that may keep her awake for hours!

Foods that have a high glycaemic index (GI), such as white pasta, white rice, potatoes, and white bread, will also create a short-term surge of energy, and may cause your child to wake in the night, feeling hungry, so you may want to avoid giving your little one any high-GI foods too close to her bedtime.

PREPARATION TIME 10 MINUTES | COOKING TIME 3 HOURS | MAKES 6–8 CHILD PORTIONS, DEPENDING ON APPETITE

mummy's chicken soup

Even if chicken soup doesn't have any proven medical benefits, a **bowlful of golden broth** is enough to comfort anyone who is feeling under the weather. **I like to add extra vegetables**, but if your child isn't keen, leave them out and serve this as chicken noodle soup.

2 chicken portions, trimmed of visible fat

1 onion, quartered

1 large carrot, peeled and cut into 4 chunks

1 parsnip, cut into 4 chunks (optional)

1 large leek, halved and washed

½ outer celery stick

1 garlic clove, peeled but left whole

3 sprigs of fresh thyme or a few parsley stalks plus 1 small bay leaf (or a bouquet garni)

5 black peppercorns

1.2 litres (2 pints) water

1 chicken or vegetable stock cube (optional)

2 tbsp frozen or canned naturally sweet sweetcorn in water, drained

2 tbsp frozen peas

30g (1oz) fine egg noodles or vermicelli

1 Put the chicken portions in a large saucepan. Add the onion, carrot, parsnip (if using), leek, celery, garlic, herbs, and peppercorns. Pour over the water and add the stock cube (if using). Bring to the boil, skimming off any froth with a slotted spoon, then reduce the heat to low, cover, and simmer very gently for 1¼ hours.

2 Strain the chicken broth into a clean pan. Reserve the chicken, carrot, and parsnip (if using); discard the remaining contents of the sieve.

3 Bring the broth back to the boil. Add the sweetcorn and peas, and crumble in the noodles. Cook for 3 minutes. Meanwhile, pull the chicken meat from the bones, discarding the skin; chop the meat. Dice the reserved carrot and parsnip. Add these to the soup. Taste and season, if necessary. Allow to cool slightly before serving.

4 The soup can be stored in the fridge for 2 days. Or freeze for up to 1 month (I prefer to freeze it without the peas and sweetcorn and add these when reheating); thaw overnight in the fridge. Reheat until boiling. Cool slightly before serving.

PREPARATION TIME 20 MINUTES | COOKING TIME 16–18 MINUTES | MAKES ABOUT 30

oat and raisin cookies

Oats are a **good source of tryptophan**, which can raise the levels of serotonin and help with sleep. Raisins are a good source of magnesium, which also **aids sleep**.

115g (4oz) butter, at room temperature

100g (3½oz) soft light brown sugar

75g (2½oz) caster sugar

1 egg, beaten

1 tsp vanilla extract

150g (5½oz) rolled oats

150g (5½oz) wholemeal or white
plain flour

½ tsp ground cinnamon

½ tsp baking powder

¼ tsp salt

125g (4½oz) raisins

1 Preheat the oven to 180°C (160°C fan), gas 4.

2 Beat the butter and the sugars together until light and fluffy. Beat in the egg and vanilla extract. Mix together the oats, flour, cinnamon, baking powder, and salt, then stir this into the butter mixture, followed by the raisins, to make a soft, slightly sticky dough.

3 Take tablespoonfuls of the cookie dough and roll into balls with dampened hands. Place the balls, spaced well apart, on two baking sheets lined with baking parchment. Flatten the balls slightly with your fingers or with a fork dusted with flour.

4 Bake the cookies for 16–18 minutes until lightly golden. Remove from the oven and leave to cool on the baking sheets for 10 minutes, then transfer to a cooling rack using a palette knife or fish slice. Allow to cool completely. The cookies will firm slightly as they cool but will still remain soft.

5 Store the cookies in an airtight tin or box. Or freeze in sealable plastic bags or boxes; thaw at room temperature for 1–2 hours when needed.

special diets for toddlers

Whether your toddler is allergic or has a specific diet for lifestyle or religious reasons, **it is perfectly possible** to present healthy, balanced meals. As long as you know where the potential nutritional shortfalls may be, **you'll have the knowledge you need** to substitute from a cornucopia of goodies.

Q Are there any meat substitutes that I can buy?

A You can buy texured vegetable protein (TVP), which is soya flour that's been processed and dried. It's available ground into granules that resemble minced beef and is prepared by mixing with vegetable stock and then leaving it to stand for a few minutes. It is great for making bolognese or burgers. As well as being a good source of protein, it is fortified with vitamin B12, which vegetarian or vegan diets sometimes lack.

★ quinoa quota

One of the very best foods you can offer a vegan toddler is quinoa. This looks like a grain but is, in fact, a seed. It is rich in essential fatty acids, protein, iron, fibre, and antioxidants. It can be used in much the same way as couscous, or can be added to soups, stews, casseroles, pasta dishes, and risottos.

Q How can I make my toddler's vegetarian menu a little more exciting?

A Vegetarian diets vary dramatically, with some vegetarians eating fish, eggs, and milk, and some cutting them out alongside meat and poultry. As long as you take care to ensure that your toddler gets the nutrients she'd normally get from eating these foods – iron, vitamin B12, protein, and zinc – anything goes.

Consider adding dairy produce, ground seeds and nuts, as well as plenty of pulses, such as chickpeas, lentils, and beans, to ensure she has adequate protein in her diet. Tofu (made from soya bean curd) doesn't have much taste but if you marinate it, you can use it to make tasty stir fries. With children under the age of five you should stick to nut butters and ground or finely chopped nuts due to the choking risk. Ground almonds make a tasty addition to cakes and crumbles. Eggs will add protein and some iron, as will fortified breakfast cereals, wholemeal bread, dried fruits, leafy green vegetables, and lentils. Most of these supply zinc, too. Vitamin B12 is adequately represented in dairy produce, fortified breakfast cereals, and eggs. You can then experiment with different herbs, spices, and other flavours (see pages 145–146).

Q What grains are a good addition to a vegan diet?

A The key is to provide variety, so the greater the number of grains you manage to include in your toddler's diet, the more nutrients he will be getting.

Good choices are quinoa (see opposite page), buckwheat (which can replace flour in most recipes), oats, corn (on its own, or in a tortilla, pasta, or even bread), wheat, wild rice, rye, brown rice, and amaranth are all worth trying, either in baking or as an addition to a healthy meal.

★ culinary adventures

Having a child with special dietary needs may force you to become a little more creative in your cooking, and to experiment with foods with which you may not be familiar. However, in the long run, your whole family will benefit from the wealth of new ingredients you explore, and will undoubtedly become more adventurous eaters, as a result.

Q What can I use instead of eggs in my allergic toddler's diet?

A Eggs are a good source of protein, and contain mainly vitamins A, D, and E. While eggs are not essential, you will need to ensure that your toddler gets protein from other sources, such as pulses, wholegrains, meat and fish, seeds, soya, and dairy produce.

Although nuts are a good source of protein, around 20–30 per cent of egg allergics have nut allergies. Multiple allergies do often rule many of these foods out, so you will need the help of a dietitian to make sure your toddler's needs are met. A diet that is rich in fresh fruit and vegetables will supply adequate vitamins and minerals, and making sure that your toddler gets plenty of wholegrains (see above) will keep her B vitamin levels topped up.

If you are baking, there are some good "egg replacers" on the market, although these will not have the same nutritional benefits as real eggs. If you are stuck for breakfast ideas, consider tofu scramble, which is a good, healthy alternative that I like to make.

Q How can I incorporate pulses into my toddler's vegetarian diet?

A On their own, most pulses are fairly bland, which makes them ideal for adding to almost any dish. A handful of cooked lentils, chickpeas, butter beans, kidney beans, or soya beans can be added to pasta dishes, vegetables bakes, and casseroles. They can often form the basis of meals, too, for example the Vegetarian shepherd's pie recipe (see overleaf), which uses lentils instead of meat. Chickpeas can be added to couscous for a cold or hot main meal, along with chopped onions, feta cheese, and some diced tomatoes. Purée chickpeas or even butter beans with some tahini, lemon juice, and garlic to make a healthy hummus to spread on toast. Try mashing butter beans with a little vegetarian stock as an alternative to mashed potatoes.

PREPARATION TIME 10 MINUTES | COOKING TIME 1 HOUR 35 MINUTES | MAKES 4–6 SMALL PIES

vegetarian shepherd's pie

Lentils are a **good source of protein and iron** for vegetarians, and green lentils in a tomato sauce makes a **savoury and satisfying filling** for these little potato-topped pies.

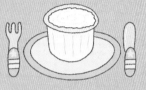

1 tbsp olive oil

1 red onion, finely chopped

1 carrot, peeled and grated

1 garlic clove, crushed

150g (5½oz) green lentils, rinsed

400g (14oz) can chopped tomatoes

600ml (1 pint) vegetable stock

150ml (5fl oz) water

2 tbsp tomato purée

1 tbsp soy sauce

1 tbsp soft light brown sugar

Freshly ground black pepper

5 tbsp frozen peas (optional)

Topping

750g (1lb 10oz) potatoes, peeled and cut in chunks

20g (¾oz) butter

4 tbsp milk

Beaten egg or grated Cheddar cheese

1 Heat the oil in a large saucepan and sauté the onion and carrot until softened and lightly browned. Add the garlic and cook for 1 minute. Stir in the lentils, tomatoes, stock, water, tomato purée, soy sauce, and sugar. Bring to the boil, then reduce the heat, part-cover, and simmer for about 1 hour or until the lentils are tender.

2 Meanwhile, cook the potatoes in lightly salted boiling water for about 15 minutes or until tender. Drain, then mash well with the butter and milk.

3 Season the lentils to taste with pepper and stir in the peas, if using. Divide among 4–6 ramekins or other small baking dishes. Spread the mashed potato over the lentils and mark in ridges with a fork. Cool, then chill. Or wrap in cling film and freeze; thaw overnight in the fridge when needed.

4 To cook, preheat the oven to 200°C (180°C fan), gas 6. Put the pies on a baking sheet, brush the tops with beaten egg (or sprinkle with cheese), and bake for about 30 minutes or until golden and piping hot. Allow to cool slightly and check the temperature before serving.

chapter 5

18–36 months:
eating with the family

18–36 months:
what you can expect

Your child will now be **a confident eater**, and will be able to manage almost everything she's offered, although she will probably start to exert her authority and have very specific **likes and dislikes**! She'll enjoy being **a part of family mealtimes**; make the most of her enthusiasm, and encourage her to try new foods.

Q **My toddler has become increasingly fussy and will eat only certain foods; is there a reason for this?**

A Rest assured that this is a normal stage in your toddler's development. Almost all toddlers go through a stage of becoming a little obsessive about their lives, demanding to wear certain clothing, drinking only from a specific cup, or eating just a few chosen foods.

In some ways, toddlerhood is a mini-adolescence, when children assert themselves and their independence in no small measure. Unfortunately, this often extends to their choice of food, which is clearly an emotive issue with parents and carers, and bound to get a good response.

The simplest and best way to deal with this is to ignore food fads and "statements". Continue to offer the same food you always have, and new foods too, and remove what he doesn't eat without comment. When he realizes that his efforts to rebel aren't getting any response, he's likely to give in and resume his normal eating patterns.

Q **How big is a toddler-sized serving?**

A Hold out her hand and place a few grapes in it. Can she fit three or four? That's roughly a portion, and you can use this calculation for all fruits and vegetables. A toddler-sized portion of protein (red meat, chicken, etc.) is the size of her palm, and a fish portion is the size of her hand. Obviously, some foods are eaten in bigger quantities (breakfast cereal, pasta, rice, and yogurt spring to mind), so don't become too concerned about portion sizes. As long as she is having at least five "handfuls" of fruit and vegetables a day, and several servings of healthy carbohydrates and protein, you're doing well.

Q **How can I encourage my child to eat a varied diet?**

A The key is to sit down as a family as often as possible and eat a varied diet together. If everyone is eating what's on offer, your child is more likely to do so, too.

Furthermore, it's important to continue to offer new foods over and over again, until they become familiar. Mix new foods with old favourites – try adding broccoli florets to macaroni cheese, or new vegetables such as mange tout and baby corn to stir-fries.

If he rejects foods continually, try different recipes to make the foods more appealing. Adding new foods to old favourites is a good trick, for example, adding mushrooms or sweet pepper to homemade pizza. Hiding food may seem like an odd option, but it can get little ones accustomed to unfamiliar flavours and textures. Children love my Hidden vegetable tomato sauce (see page 183), and have no idea they're eating vegetables!

sitting at the table

It's important to include your little one in family meals. She may be able to sit on a family chair with a booster seat, although it will probably take a few weeks to encourage her to stay put! Otherwise, many high chairs have removable trays so they can be pushed up to the table.

milk and other drinks

Your growing toddler **no longer needs to rely** on his "baby" milk for the nutrients that his varied diet now offers, but he may still enjoy **the comfort of regular feeds.** Breastfeeding can continue for as long as you feel comfortable. Full weaning can be a slow process, and it's best to **go at your child's pace.**

Q How much milk do children need at this age?

A The maximum amount your toddler needs is about 500ml (18fl oz), but it's important to remember that this figure should also include other dairy produce she eats. So if she gets plenty of cheese and yogurt in her diet, she'll need correspondingly less. Most toddlers who have a varied, healthy diet with lots of dairy produce can get by on about 250ml (9fl oz) per day. Some children meet their requirements from dairy produce alone.

Q Is there any nutritional value in my breast milk at this point?

A Breast milk continues to be a valuable and nutritious addition to your child's diet; it's a good balance of nutrients and although your toddler will by now be getting most of what he needs from his diet, it can help to make up any shortfalls. Moreover, breast milk contains your antibodies to disease and will help to protect your child from illness. Mothers produce antibodies to whatever disease is present in their environment, which ensures that breast milk is perfectly and individually "designed" to combat the diseases with which their children are in contact.

⭐ **did you know ...**

that warm milk will help to soothe your child to sleep? The reason is that it contains a chemical known as tryptophan, which encourages the production of serotonin (the feel-good hormone) that is responsible for enhancing sleep. It doesn't have to be warm; however, many little ones associate warm milk with comfort, companionship, and settling down for the night. Offer it in a cup rather than a bottle, to prevent damage to teeth, and try to rinse her teeth before she drifts off.

Q **I enjoy the closeness of breastfeeding my two-year-old, but it's starting to feel a bit odd; should I stop?**

A Negative emotions are often the result of concern about what other people might think of breastfeeding a toddler. Unfortunately, breastfeeding past a year appears to be frowned upon in some corners, which doesn't help.

Breastfeeding is a personal decision, and the length of time you continue should be based on how you and your toddler feel about it. If you are both enjoying the closeness, there is absolutely no reason why you should stop completely. You may, however, feel more comfortable dropping the daytime feeds, which are more likely to be in the company of others. It's worth mentioning that later weaning has positive psychological benefits, allowing your little one to outgrow infancy at her own pace, and giving her emotional security and comfort.

Q **My child still drinks a lot of milk, and isn't very hungry at meal times. How can I cut it down?**

A Firstly, make sure you're keeping to the recommended 500ml (18fl oz) a day. If he's drinking much more than this, the best thing to do is to avoid offering milk between meals. If he's still taking a bottle, move him on to a cup, and see the tips, right, on how to wean him off his night-time feed. If he is still demanding milk, try to work out what's going on. Is he hungry, thirsty, or looking for comfort? Too much milk is the most common cause of iron deficiency. Toddlers with low iron levels have a poor appetite and do not sleep well and hence demand more milk, which makes the situation even worse. See your doctor if you're concerned.

Q **How can I wean a toddler who has become reliant on her night-time feed?**

A Many babies and toddlers associate breastfeeding with sleep, and it's important to try to break this link. But go slowly, as gradual weaning tends to work best. Many experts support the "never offer but never refuse" school of thought, which means changing your routine so that breastfeeding is no longer "on offer", but equally, remaining open to responding to your toddler's needs. It's best to start when there are no other changes afoot such as potty training or starting childcare, as children are more needy in times of change.

Try to ensure, also, that your little one isn't hungry or thirsty at bedtime. Offer a bedtime snack an hour or so before bed, with some water or milk.

It's also worth talking to your little one. While she won't understand completely what's going on, you can explain that she won't be having mummy's milk at bedtime anymore because she is a big girl now, but that she can have proper drinks in her special cup instead. Show delight and pride, too, when she goes for an evening without a feed.

Offer distractions at bedtime, such as curling up together with a book, away from the bedroom. Spending time together will compensate for the loss of closeness of breastfeeding.

⭐ a "grown-up" cup?

From about 2½ to 3 years, most children have adequate hand-eye co-ordination to get at least some of the contents of a lidless cup into their mouths, but be prepared for spills. You can most certainly offer one earlier, but you'll need to help him with it, and keep a cloth handy to mop up spills! A little advice: when you're out and about or away from the kitchen, it's probably best to keep the lid on. If he resists, try putting his drink in a small bottle with a sports cap, which is much more "grown up".

Q Should I be offering water only between meals?

A Because of the risk that fruit juice and sweetened drinks pose to teeth, it is a good idea to offer water only. Water is the perfect way to keep your little one hydrated, and goes to work as soon as it enters her body, whereas fruit juices and even squashes have to be "digested" before beginning the hydration process. Water encourages healthy digestion and increases the flow of saliva, which both protects and remineralizes teeth, and makes the digestive process more efficient. It also ensures that she has more energy, and that her immune system works efficiently. See page 129 for ways to encourage your little one to drink more water.

Q What should my child be served to drink with meals?

A Sipping water or a little diluted fruit juice during mealtimes is fine, although it's important to remember that little tummies fill up quickly and if your child drinks too much, he's likely to eat less, which may mean an inadequate intake of nutrients. Milk can prevent iron from being efficiently extracted from food, so is best offered after a meal, rather than during. For similar reasons, diluted fruit juice is suggested, because vitamin C encourages the uptake of iron from food.

Q My child drinks juice throughout the day – will this harm her teeth?

A Sipping on juice means that her teeth are constantly being bathed in sugars that can encourage tooth decay. It's much better to serve fruit juice with meals, or at a set snack time, when the other foods on offer can help to neutralize the sugars and acids. It's best to offer water between meals (see left), but if she does have fruit juice, encourage her to rinse her mouth with water afterwards.

Q Are flavoured waters or milks appropriate?

A The single greatest advantage to flavoured waters is that they tend to be more appealing to kids. It's undoubtedly easier to get little ones to drink more water if it doesn't taste like water. Look out for brands with a little added fruit juice or fruit juice concentrate, and avoid those that contain sugar or artificial sweeteners. Flavoured milks are normally high in sugar and artificial flavourings and additives, so should be avoided.

meals without tears

As your toddler begins to **exert her authority** in all areas of her life, she will soon cotton on to the idea that food is an emotive issue, and that she'll get a good reaction if she **refuses some foods**, and demands others. Most toddlers experience periods of faddy eating; **remain calm**, and continue to offer the foods you want her to eat.

Q My toddler picks out the vegetables, from his meals. What can I do?

A Lots of little ones seem to have an inbuilt radar when it comes to pinpointing any trace of vegetables, and sometimes fruit, in food. It may be that kids instinctively know that we want them to eat fruit and vegetables, and therefore use them as a tool to exercise their will and right to make their own choices, on the road to independence. My advice is to get crafty!

You can disguise vegetables by blending them into a tomato sauce, and serving with pasta (see page 183), or try adding puréed vegetables to soups, stews, and casseroles. It's a good idea to leave a few "chunks", allowing your toddler the satisfaction of picking them out before unwittingly consuming more. You can sneak veggies into wraps, cannelloni, lasagne, quesadillas, or under grated cheese on pizza. Mix puréed butternut squash into a cheese sauce to make a nutrient-packed macaroni cheese, or mash carrots into mashed potato for a delicious cottage pie topping. Some children also prefer raw vegetables, like cucumber sticks or strips of sweet pepper. Finally, try him with vegetables that he hasn't seen before that perhaps look more fun than a plate of broccoli, such as baby corn or asparagus.

Q My toddler will only eat plain foods with no sauces; can you think of ways to tempt her?

A Sometimes "dips" are more popular than sauces, so offering her pasta sauce in a separate bowl into which she can dip her pasta shapes may appeal, or a peanut sauce for her chicken skewers may work well. Many kids like to see their food separated on the plate, and in its simplest form. This doesn't necessarily mean they don't like sauces, it just means that they like things plain, obvious, and simple, and they like to know exactly what is on their plates. Try putting her sauce on the side, and she may try a little.

There is no reason, however, that your toddler's food has to be bland. You can marinate fish, chicken, and tofu to give it wonderful flavours, and use all sorts of different herbs and spices.

★ multi-vitamins?

The Department of Health reommends vitamin drops for all under-twos (see page 152). It's a good idea to continue to give your child a multi-vitamin and mineral tablet or liquid if he is a fussy eater, as it will contain a little of all of the nutrients he needs for growth and development. "Drops" may be your best bet, because they reduce the potential risk of choking. If you go for chewable tablets, avoid those with sugar or artificial sweeteners.

Q How can I "hide" vegetables when my toddler will eat only plain food?

A It's obviously much more difficult when you are unable to purée or finely chop vegetables and other healthy foods into sauces. However, it's not impossible!

Try "stuffing" her chicken breast with cheese and spinach or other vegetables, or adding puréed or chopped vegetables to fish or chicken balls, which can be breaded and cooked. Purée vegetables into "dipping" sauces, or add grated vegetables to beef or chicken mince to make tasty meatballs (see page 216). Add grated or chopped vegetables to scrambled eggs, quiches, omelettes, and even cakes and muffins. Every little bit you manage to get into your toddler will make a difference.

Q Should I ever force my child to eat something she refuses?

A It's never a good idea to force-feed a child, not only because it brings a confrontational, negative element to food and eating, which should be associated with fun and pleasure, but because it can, in extreme cases, lead to serious problems with food, including phobias. Furthermore, if you force your child, you are telling him that you are anxious about what he's eating, which gives him the ammunition he needs to use food as a weapon.

Involving your little one in family meals can help him to broaden his palate, as he'll want to do what everyone else is doing. Sometimes suggesting "just one spoonful" of everything or, indeed, giving one "veto" – the choice of one food he doesn't have to eat – will make him feel empowered enough to do as requested.

A reward sticker chart in the kitchen is also a good idea – give him a sticker for every new food he tries, and when he has a certain amount of stickers, he gets a small reward.

Q Should I allow my toddler to decide what she will eat?

A There is no harm in giving choices to your toddler, but only when she is encouraged to choose between several healthy options that you want her to eat. Giving her free rein will probably lead to a diet of biscuits, crisps, and chocolate milk. You can, however, diffuse a tricky situation by allowing her to choose which of the three vegetables on offer she wants to eat, or getting her involved in the planning of meals to some extent: shall we have broccoli or peas tonight? This empowers children and can encourage them to eat food they wouldn't normally eat.

Q My child will only eat fruit if it's cooked; does it still have some nutritional value?

A Vitamins and minerals, in particular vitamin C, are easily destroyed when food is cooked at high heat, so your child won't be getting quite as much as he would if he was eating fresh fruit as well. However, some nutrition is better than none, and as long as he is getting a variety of different cooked fruits, this is fine in the short term. One positive thing about serving cooked fruit is that you can normally blend several together, thereby increasing the overall number of different nutrients. Try to lightly steam fruit rather than boiling, or perhaps bake it in a foil wrapper, which helps to preserve nutrients to some extent.

Continue to offer fresh fruit alongside – perhaps making it look more appealing by creating exotic fruit platters with a yogurt and honey dip, or making melon balls, or serving kiwi fruit in an egg cup. Encourage your child to help you make smoothies, which offer a fantastic boost of fresh-fruit nutrients (see page 205). Also make fresh fruit ice lollies (see page 116) or banana ice cream together (see page 119) for some tasty treats that are incredibly healthy too.

Q How can I make fish more appealing?

A At first, kids tend to enjoy white fish, such as cod, sole, and plaice. Once your little one becomes accustomed to the flavour and texture, you can move on to more flavourful oily fish. All fish is healthy, but oily fish, such as salmon, sardines, and fresh tuna, is the healthiest for kids, because of the high levels of omega oils now known to improve health and behaviour on many levels.

Fish can be poached, flaked, breaded and served as goujons (see page 138), or minced and served in little balls. Fish pies are a favourite with little ones, especially if served in individual ramekins. Stir tinned tuna into pasta sauces, or use as a sandwich filling. You may need to cover fish with a lemon or hollandaise sauce, or even cheese or ketchup to encourage your little one to try it. Whatever you do, make sure you remove all scales and bones – you don't want to put her off for good!

★ did you know ...

that it can take up to 10 times for a food to become "familiar"? Before this, children may reject it completely, or experiment a little by touching or smelling it, and even licking it or putting bits in their mouths before spitting them out. This is all part of the process of acclimatization. Continue to offer the food until he shows interest. Be patient, though, and remember that we all have foods we dislike; as long as he's eating more than he's rejecting, he'll be fine.

Q How can I tempt my toddler to eat breakfast?

A Toddlers often wake bursting with energy and desperate to get on with a new day. Stopping for breakfast can seem boring, no matter how hungry they are! A fast of 12 or 14 hours may simply not be enough to encourage your toddler to the table, when there is much to do.

The best advice is to offer a little play time, and give him some choices. He may not be hungry at the time, but he'll be more likely to eat something he has decided he wants to eat. A yogurt and fruit smoothie, alongside a few squares of peanut butter on toast or a handful of dry breakfast cereal is fine (the Maple oat clusters recipe on page 186 is perfect for this). If he chooses the fruit for his smoothie, he may also be more inclined to drink it. There's also no reason why breakfast has to include traditional breakfast foods. A ham and cheese, or egg mayonnaise sandwich with a glass of fruit juice, is perfectly acceptable, as is a little of last night's pizza or pasta. Serve his favourites. As long as they are balanced and healthy, they'll give him enough fuel to get through the morning.

Q How can I encourage my child to eat foods that aren't "soft"?

A Some kids are late "chewers", and are just learning to control the muscles in their mouth; others may be late teethers (or getting a new crop of teeth, in particular, molars), which can make chewing uncomfortable. Make sure you continue to offer plenty of finger foods; if she becomes accustomed to a mix of different textures from her finger foods, she'll soon be able to manage main meals. Slowly add soft lumps, such as a little rice or tiny pasta shapes, to her regular meals, so that she learns to manage them. If she regularly chokes or gags, it's worth seeing your doctor for reassurance.

Q Is there any way to introduce foods with more unusual textures?

A Toddlers can be notoriously fussy about things that don't look or taste familiar. For example, fairly bland foods such as mushrooms can produce horror because the consistency is unusual. Similarly, stringy foods like celery and some cuts of beef can cause problems, as can crunchier foods such as brown rice, chopped nuts, and seeds.

The best thing to do is to continue to offer a wide variety of foods with different textures. Offer raw fruits and vegetables with tasty dips, and swap over to a crunchy peanut butter rather than smooth to accustom him to chew and swallow pieces of nuts. Gradually is a key word, and it does help to finely chop problem foods, such as seeds and nuts, at first. Once again, finger foods are the perfect way to provide a variety of different textures. Mixing flavours can also help to encourage the process; for example, mashing bananas with avocado, or adding dried fruit to a favourite yogurt.

PREPARATION TIME 10 MINUTES | COOKING TIME 26 MINUTES | MAKES 8 CHILD PORTIONS

hidden vegetable tomato sauce

Tomato sauce is so versatile and I always keep a stash of it in my freezer to use **with pasta, chicken, or fish, or on pizzas**. As this is puréed, no one will ever know that vegetables are hidden in it.

1 tbsp olive oil

1 red onion, chopped

1 small carrot, grated

½ small courgette, grated

¼ small red pepper, chopped

¼ eating apple such as Pink Lady, cored and grated

1 garlic clove, crushed

2 x 400g (14oz) cans chopped tomatoes

2 tbsp tomato purée

1 tbsp sun-dried tomato purée

¼ tsp dried oregano

1 tsp caster sugar

Salt and freshly ground black pepper

1 Heat the olive oil in a large saucepan and gently cook the onion, carrot, courgette, red pepper, and apple for about 5 minutes or until softened but not browned, stirring occasionally. Add the garlic and cook for 1 minute.

2 Add the remaining ingredients. Bring to the boil, then reduce the heat, part-cover, and simmer gently for about 20 minutes or until thick and all the vegetables are tender. Stir from time to time.

3 Purée the sauce in a blender or food processor. Season to taste with salt and pepper. Cool and chill, or freeze in individual portions; when needed, thaw at room temperature. Reheat until piping hot, then cool slightly before serving.

PREPARATION TIME 15 MINUTES | COOKING TIME 6–10 MINUTES, PLUS PASTA COOKING | MAKES 4 CHILD PORTIONS

funny-face beef burgers

Your **own yummy burgers** will be better than any fast food, and you and your children can have **lots of fun decorating the burgers with silly faces**. Or serve the burgers more traditionally in buns.

1 tbsp olive oil

1 large shallot, finely chopped

¼ apple, peeled, cored, and grated

½ small garlic clove, crushed

1 tsp balsamic vinegar

¼ tsp fresh thyme or chopped parsley

2 tsp clear honey

150g (5½oz) extra lean minced beef

2 tbsp grated Parmesan cheese

1 tbsp tomato ketchup

1 tsp oyster sauce

20g (¾oz) fresh breadcrumbs

Sunflower oil, for frying

To decorate: peas and a mini
    cherry tomato

Per portion:

30g (1oz) spaghetti or macaroni

3 tbsp tomato sauce (see pages 98 or
    183, or use good-quality bought sauce)

1 Heat the oil in a small frying pan and soften the shallot and apple for 2 minutes. Add the garlic and cook for 1 minute. Add the vinegar and cook, stirring, until evaporated, then stir in the thyme and honey. Transfer to a bowl and cool slightly. Add the remaining ingredients to the bowl and mix together. Shape into four burgers. Cover and chill until needed. Or wrap individually and freeze for up to 1 month; thaw overnight in the fridge.

2 To cook, heat a little oil in a large non-stick frying pan and cook the burgers over a moderate heat for 3–4 minutes per side until cooked through. At the same time, cook the pasta according to packet instructions; drain and toss with the tomato sauce.

3 Arrange some pasta on a plate to resemble hair (spaghetti for straight, macaroni for curls) and set the burgers under the hair. Add peas for eyes and a mini cherry tomato for a nose (or use carrot or tomato ketchup). For the mouth, use a curved piece of pasta (or tomato or red pepper). Serve any leftover pasta in a separate dish.

PREPARATION TIME 5 MINUTES | COOKING TIME 50–55 MINUTES | MAKES 6–8 CHILD PORTIONS

maple-oat clusters

It's easy to make your own **delicious breakfast cereal** with oats, **pecans, and maple syrup,** and this will keep in an airtight container for several weeks. It's also good sprinkled over fresh fruit or plain yogurt, **or just nibbled as a snack.**

175g (6oz) jumbo rolled oats

30g (1oz) chopped pecan nuts

¼ tsp salt

85g (3oz) soft light brown sugar

4 tbsp maple syrup

85g (3oz) butter, at room temperature

1 Preheat the oven to 180°C (160°C fan), gas 4.

2 Put the oats, nuts, salt, and sugar in a bowl and stir until well combined. Add the syrup and softened butter and mix with a wooden spoon, then draw together with your hands to form a ball.

3 Press the oat mixture out on a non-stick baking sheet, to make a disc about 1cm (½in) thick. Press down well to compact the oats.

4 Bake for about 20 minutes or until lightly golden, then use a metal spoon to gently separate the oat disc into large clumps (the centre will still be very soft). Return to the oven and bake for a further 10–15 minutes. Gently move the clumps around, then bake for a final 10 minutes or until the clumps are golden. Remove from the oven and leave them to cool on the baking sheet (they will crisp up more as they cool).

5 Gently break any larger clumps into bite-sized pieces. Store the clusters in an airtight box.

healthy, but not boring

A healthy diet is crucially important to your child's health, development, growth and wellbeing, and it is important to ensure that he is getting **all the nutrients he needs** in the form of healthy, regular meals. But healthy doesn't mean boring! Tempt your child with **fun, delicious meals**.

Q What is the most important part of a child's diet?

A There is no single most important part, as every element combines to produce the right balance of nutrients he needs to grow and develop, and to achieve and maintain good health. Every child needs fats, carbohydrates, protein, fibre, and vitamins and minerals, and all are equally essential.

The key is balance and variety. Balance simply means getting some of each food group in every meal; vitamins and minerals are easily covered by including fresh fruit and vegetables, and good-quality wholegrains such as pulses and wholemeal bread, brown rice, and pasta.

The second element is variety. The greater the variety of foods you choose, the greater the number of nutrients. So try thinking outside the box a little. Offer a sweet potato rather than a traditional white potato, or some corn pasta in place of your normal white varieties. Choose brightly coloured fruits and vegetables, and mix and match them at each different meal. Offer raw vegetables and a dip or a platter of fruit chunks as snacks. Grate courgettes and carrots into sauces, and add pumpkin or sunflower seeds to cookies or granola. If every meal is slightly different, you'll be doing a great job.

Q At what age should I start teaching my child about good nutrition?

A It's never too early to teach children about good nutrition. From the earliest days, you can discuss various ingredients, and talk about why they are good: fish makes your brain grow and makes you very clever; berries make you strong and healthy with not so many colds and coughs; porridge makes you super-energetic and you'll be able to run around all morning; cheese, milk and yogurt make your bones and teeth strong … that sort of thing.

Then use specific examples to help drive the messages home. For example, if she's tired after a hyper high following a birthday party, explain that sugar makes us super energetic for a while, but makes us tired and headachey later on. It doesn't mean lecturing kids, simply using every opportunity to explain why good foods matters.

Q What are some good ideas for dips to go with raw fruits and vegetables?

A Dips are a great way to encourage little ones to eat more fruit, and, in particular, vegetables.

Hummus, taramasalata, and tzaziki are all good choices for raw vegetables, or try stirring a teaspoon of pesto into a little plain yogurt or mayonnaise. Even a tablespoon of ketchup mixed with the same amount of mayonnaise makes a delightful pink dip that will appeal to little ones. Sour cream or crème fraiche with chives is usually popular and will entice your little one to pick up the veggies.

For fruit, honey, fruit yogurt, fromage frais, or even a little maple syrup make tasty dips. One of my favourite combinations for a tasty dip for fruit is 3 tbsp Greek yogurt, 1 tsp milk, 1 tsp icing sugar, and 1 tsp lemon curd. Cinnamon and apple purée or a good-quality shop-bought fruit compôte added to plain yogurt are delcious too.

Q I've heard that wholegrains are best. What are some good ways to encourage my child to eat wholegrains?

A Wholegrains, or foods made from them, contain all the essential parts and naturally occurring nutrients of the entire grain. Wholegrains are not refined; nothing has been stripped or removed from the grains. So wholemeal bread is a wholegrain, while white bread is not. They are rich in vitamins B and E, the minerals magnesium, selenium, and zinc, fibre, and other valuable nutrients that have been shown to protect against many health conditions, and encourage optimum health and nutrition.

The question is which grains, and how! Most little ones like corn, and it can be eaten on its own or mixed into stews, soups, and even sandwich fillings. There are some interesting wholegrain rices about, including red and wild rice (which is, in fact, a grass) that can appeal to toddlers because they are rather exotic looking. Stir a little barley into soups or casseroles, use buckwheat or corn pastas occasionally, and choose wholegrain breads, such as wholewheat, oat, and millet for more variety. Quinoa can be served rather like couscous, or stirred into couscous or added to salads for extra crunch.

★ did you know ...

that raw fruit and vegetables contain a powerful antioxidant called glutathione that helps to detoxify your child's body? It encourages healthy elimination and sticks to the nasty bits in your child's gut, and then escorts them out! New research also suggests that this antioxidant is crucial for a healthy immune system. Just one more reason to offer fresh fruits and vegetables to your little one throughout the day. Cut them into bite-sized finger foods for a healthy snack.

snacks and treats

Snacks and treats don't have to be unhealthy to be tempting and delicious, and with **the right ingredients**, they can form a nutritious and integral part of your child's well-balanced diet. Used judiciously, too, they **add important variety** to your child's diet, and encourage little ones to experiment with **a wider range of flavours**.

Q How important are snacks? My child simply can't make it between meals without something to eat.

A Snacks can be very important for some toddlers who will struggle to make it between main meals without something to eat. The reason is that their tummies are small, and they can't get adequate calories in one sitting to see them through long periods without something to eat. They all need some refuelling, and it is healthy to encourage them to eat when they are hungry, so that they learn to understand and respond to "hunger cues". Many children with weight problems never experience the feeling of being hungry, and are encouraged to eat constantly, and to clean their plates. You'll be doing your toddler a favour to allow her to pick and choose from a snack plate, and to eat according to her own needs.

The secret is to schedule your snacks so that they don't run too close to mealtimes (which can be counterproductive, as your toddler won't be hungry enough to eat properly, and will demand more snacks afterwards), to offer healthy food that doesn't detract from the nutritional value of her overall diet (see page 190 for ideas), and to avoid "grazing" (a constant succession of snacks between meals).

Q Should I allow my child to help himself to snacks when he is hungry?

A Yes, and no. Most certainly allow him to choose from a selection of snacks at the appropriate time, but make sure you give a choice of things that you actually want him to eat.

Helping himself whenever he is hungry, however, is not a good idea. First of all, it can lead to unhealthy grazing, which means that he won't have an appetite for meals, and it can also lead to overeating – choosing food for comfort, or eating when he's actually thirsty rather than hungry.

It's good practice to allow older kids to choose one or two snacks from a "healthy" snack drawer or shelf in the fridge, during pre-arranged times, as it encourages them to make healthy choices and to eat only when they are hungry. Toddlers, however, do not have the maturity to make sensible choices, and won't understand that a little might be enough to satisfy them.

★ more snack ideas

- Breadsticks with cream cheese
- Rice cakes or a little dried cereal
- Fromage frais
- Chunks of cheese
- Dried fruit
- Toasted pitta bread with hummus
- Smoothies (see page 205)
- Fresh fruit and vegetables with dips (see page 188)
- Fruit ice lollies (see page 116)
- Fresh muffins
- Mini sandwiches (see opposite)
- Bread with a little butter

Q Does excess sugar make it harder for my child to sleep?

A Most definitely. First of all, sugar causes a "blood sugar" rush, which means that she will experience a burst of energy (appearing hyperactive, even), followed by a slump, which leaves her tearful, tired, and even withdrawn. So sugary foods eaten near to bedtime will discourage settling down to sleep; however, if she's had them a couple of hours in advance, she may collapse into bed in exhaustion. But that doesn't mean that offering sugary foods is a good way to ensure sleep later on. High sugar intake can cause restless sleep, as your child's body struggles to adjust the insulin required to deal with what she's eaten.

Q At what age can I offer sweets?

A The longer you leave it, the better, as you will put off the inevitable demands that occur from the minute your toddler has her first taste! It's important to remember that toddlers have small tummies, and even a tiny packet of sweets can fill them up with empty calories, and prevent them from eating a healthy meal or snack. Sweets also cause tooth decay, which can affect even milk teeth.

There is no real reason why sweets of any nature need to be introduced before the age of two. However, once your toddler starts nursery school or playgroup, or spends time with other children on play dates or in childcare, he may not agree! Peer pressure occurs in even the tiniest tots, and most kids want to eat what their friends are eating.

There is no reason why you have to give in, and you can most certainly explain why you don't want your toddler to eat certain foods, but the day of reckoning is on the horizon and he'll undoubtedly have his first tastes soon. For this reason, it's a good idea to introduce them yourself, first, and to establish your family view on sweets. Some families have a "sweet" jar, and allow one after dinner on the weekend, perhaps, which gives a little one something to look forward to, and also makes it clear that they aren't "everyday" foods. Similarly, bake a treat together, such as jam tarts (see page 193), and impress the idea that this is a special treat. You can also offer some healthier alternatives to sweets, such as yogurt-covered raisins or dried fruit pieces in child-friendly packets.

Make treats occasional. Diets high in sugar are also often high in fat and low in fibre. If your child fills up on sugary and fatty foods, he is likely to be at risk of vitamin and mineral deficiencies and at risk of obesity, heart disease, and diabetes in later life.

sandwiches for toddlers

You can **add more texture** for this age group, but not too many bits. Flatten the slices of bread with a rolling pin before buttering them lightly – thinner sandwiches are **easier for toddlers to hold** and eat.

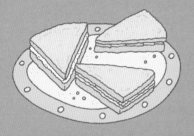

egg and chive sandwich

★ Lower 1 egg into a saucepan of boiling water and simmer for 12 minutes. Immediately rinse with plenty of cold water, then peel off the shell. Mash the egg with 2 tsp mayonnaise, 2–3 snipped fresh chives, and a little seasoning. Use to fill one or more sandwiches.

double cheese sandwich

★ Spread cream cheese over one slice of bread and scatter on 30g (1oz) grated Cheddar cheese. Sandwich with the second slice of bread.

peanut butter-banana sandwich

★ Spread 1 tbsp peanut butter (smooth or crunchy) over one slice of bread, then top with ½ small mashed banana. Add the second slice of bread.

sardine and tomato sandwich

★ Mash 1 or 2 canned sardines over one slice of bread (be sure to remove any bones) and spread with 1–2 tsp tomato ketchup. Top with the second slice of bread.

cottage cheese-pineapple sandwich

★ Scoop this from a tub and use to fill a sandwich.

PREPARATION TIME 30 MINUTES PLUS 1 HOUR RESTING | COOKING TIME 15 MINUTES | MAKES 24

mini jam tarts

It's fun for children to make **mini treats** like jam tarts as they can be involved in the whole process: **making the pastry**, rolling it out, **cutting the circles** and pushing them into tins, and spooning in the filling. For a richer pastry, add an egg yolk and use slightly less water.

250g (9oz) plain flour, plus extra for rolling

125g (4½oz) butter, diced

Pinch of salt

2–3 tbsp iced water

8 tbsp high-fruit strawberry spread with no added sugar

1 Put the flour and salt in a bowl, add the butter, and rub in with your fingertips until the mixture looks like fine breadcrumbs. Add 2 tbsp water and stir with a palette knife, adding more water a little at a time until the mixture will just hold together without crumbling when squeezed lightly. Flatten the dough into a disc. If possible, wrap in cling film and rest in the fridge for 1 hour.

2 Preheat the oven to 200°C (180°C fan), gas 6. Roll out the dough on a lightly floured surface until quite thin and cut out about 24 circles with a 5cm (2in) fluted round cutter. Gather up the trimmings and re-roll as necessary. Carefully press the dough circles into the holes of two tartlet tins.

3 Put 1 tsp of strawberry spread in each pastry case. Bake for about 15 minutes or until the pastry is golden. Leave to cool in the tins for 5 minutes, then transfer to a wire rack to cool completely. Store in an airtight container.

4 To freeze, put the cooled tarts in a single layer in a resealable box and freeze; when needed, thaw at room temperature for 1–2 hours.

out and about

As your child becomes more independent, she'll be able to enjoy an increasing number of **outings with family and friends**, and may **begin to eat meals outside** her home. It's natural to be concerned that she's getting everything she needs, but keeping your eye on the overall picture, and using **a little creativity**, will help.

Q What are good restaurant options for little children?

A Given the opportunity, many little ones are very adventurous eaters and will try foods from many different cultures. In fact, eating out can encourage them to try things you may have no luck in serving at home.

Thai food is fun, and many dishes are fragrant rather than spicy, with lots of vegetables, noodles, and rice served alongside. Pizza is perfectly healthy as long as you stick to vegetable toppings, thin crust – and don't overdo the cheese! Even grilled beef or chicken burgers, made from 100 per cent meat, are fine. Traditional favourites such as vegetable-based pasta dishes, fish or shepherd's pies, or even roast dinners are good choices.

In reality, anything goes, as long as you avoid anything that is very fatty, high in salt, and high in sugar, or which contains artificial colours, flavourings or additives such as MSG (often found in Chinese dishes).

Q Are there any healthy alternatives to fast foods?

A First of all, there is no reason why you can't prepare healthy fast food in your own home. Burgers made with lean meat are delicious (see page 185), and you can make your own "chips" by blanching sweet potato and potato wedges for a few minutes, brushing them with olive oil, and roasting until golden brown. See page 198, too, for healthy alternatives to chicken nuggets.

Vegetable pizzas created with light homemade bases, such as split toasted English muffins, topped with fresh vegetables, tomato sauce, and a sprinkling of cheese, are far superior to store-bought and takeaway alternatives. You can easily create chicken skewers by marinating chunks of chicken in any number of ingredients such as lemon juice, honey and soy sauce, or olive oil, lemon, garlic, and fresh thyme. Stir-fries are great fast food, and the vegetables are lightly cooked, so retain most of their nutrients. Baked potatoes with easy-to-prepare toppings, such as baked beans or tuna-mayonnaise make a healthy, family-friendly meal too.

Q My child is more adventurous with his food now; can you suggest some exciting packed lunch ideas?

A The first thing to consider is that your child's packed lunch represents a meal, and should be as nutritionally balanced as any meal, with protein, carbohydrates, vegetables, and fruit appearing in some form or another.

Small bite-sized sandwiches are always popular, (see page 191 for filling suggestions) and if you use wholemeal, half-and-half, or multi-seed bread, she'll get even more nutrients. Wraps make a nice change – fill them with chicken or prawns and salad.

If your child is adept with a fork, you can create mini salads, which are a good alternative to sandwiches. Add chunks of chicken, halved cherry tomatoes, and snipped chives to a potato salad, or make a pasta salad with pasta twirls, turkey, and broccoli, and a delicious dressing (3 tbsp light olive oil, 1 tbsp balsamic vingear, 1 tbsp soy sauce, and ½ tsp caster sugar).

Raw vegetables are often more appealing and easier to manage in lunchboxes, and you can provide a selection with a little pot of hummus. Miniature fish or chicken balls with a little pot of ketchup or sweet and sour sauce for dipping are nutritious and fun, too.

Little pots of yogurt, miniature cheeses, and cartons of cream cheese with breadsticks will provide a boost of calcium.

Smoothies or fruit juices, plus small containers of fruit chunks or berries, and tiny boxes of raisins or other dried fruits, yogurt-covered raisins, individual portions of fruit purée, and dried fruit bars are good ways to encourage your little one to eat fruit. Mini muffins (see page 197) and oatmeal raisin cookies (see page 167) make ideal homemade desserts.

Q What should we take along to keep our fussy toddler happy on holiday?

A Some children are aghast to find that their firm favourites are not available on holiday, and may struggle to find something on the menu.

Snacking doesn't tend to be as popular in some countries, so if your toddler gets by with regular small snacks and meals, you may want to consider bringing along individual packets of breadsticks, raisins and other dried fruit, mini pots of yeast extract or peanut butter, and rice cakes. But don't panic; you can easily get good-quality bread, fruit and vegetables in most countries, and most places will offer rice, noodles, or pasta, and serve it plain as requested. However, you may well be surprised how much your toddler enjoys eating some of the ethnic-style food, such as noodles, paella, or curries. Many toddlers eat better when they're away from their usual routine.

★ rushed mornings

If you need to give your little one breakfast on the go, good ideas include: little sandwiches (see page 191); a mini, muffin (see page 197); a tub of fruit chunks with squeezy yogurt on the side; toast fingers with hummus; peanut butter or fruit purée; or even cereal in a plastic bag with raisins and other dried fruits.

PREPARATION TIME 20 MINUTES | COOKING TIME 25–30 MINUTES | MAKES 12

apple-bran muffins

These muffins are **full of good things** like raisins, apple, and bran flakes. They're great for a **breakfast on the go**, but be sure to supervise your little ones when they are eating. For **easier-to-hold mini muffins**, bake in 24 petit four cases for 12–15 minutes.

100g (3½oz) bran flakes

5 tbsp milk

150g (5½oz) apple purée (homemade or from a jar)

1 egg

1 tsp vanilla extract

100g (3½oz) soft light brown sugar

100ml (3½fl oz) sunflower oil

115g (4oz) wholemeal flour

2 tsp baking powder

¼ tsp bicarbonate of soda

1½ tsp ground cinnamon

Pinch of salt (optional)

75g (2½ oz) raisins

1 tbsp demerara sugar

1 Preheat the oven to 180°C (160°C fan), gas 4. Line a small muffin or tartlet tin with 12 paper cases.

2 Crush the bran flakes into a large bowl. Add the milk and apple purée, stir well, and leave to soak for 10 minutes. Meanwhile, whisk together the egg, vanilla extract, brown sugar, and oil.

3 Add the egg mixture to the bran mixture and stir together. Sift over the flour, baking powder, bicarbonate of soda, 1 tsp of the cinnamon, and the salt, if using, adding any residue from the sieve. Fold in, along with the raisins. Divide the mixture among the paper cases (an ice-cream scoop is good for this). The cases will be almost full.

4 Mix together the demerara sugar and remaining ½ tsp ground cinnamon and sprinkle over the muffins. Bake for 25–30 minutes until risen and firm to the touch. Cool in the tin for 5 minutes, then transfer to a wire rack to cool completely.

5 Store in an airtight box for 2 days. Or freeze in a resealable plastic bag or box; thaw at room temperature for 1–2 hours when needed.

PREPARATION TIME 20 MINUTES PLUS MARINATING | COOKING TIME 6–8 MINUTES | MAKES 8 CHILD PORTIONS

tender chicken fingers

Chicken fingers are **better for small children** to bite into than big nuggets and a marinade helps to **tenderize the chicken**, making it **easy to chew**. I find that puffed rice cereal is a very tasty coating.

2 small skinless, boneless chicken breasts, cut into little finger-size strips

3–4 tbsp sunflower oil, for frying

Marinade

6 tbsp milk

4 tbsp plain low-fat yogurt

1 tsp lemon juice

1 tsp Worcestershire sauce

¼ tsp dried oregano

½ tsp fresh thyme leaves or ¼ tsp dried thyme

¼ tsp paprika

Coating

55g (2oz) puffed rice cereal

30g (1oz) Parmesan cheese, grated

¼ tsp dried oregano

1 egg

1 tsp water

3 tbsp plain flour

1 Mix the marinade ingredients in a large bowl. Add the chicken, cover, and leave to marinate in the fridge for a minimum of 2 hours, or overnight.

2 Put the cereal, Parmesan, and oregano in a food processor and process briefly to crumbs. Spread the crumbs out on a large plate. Beat the egg in a bowl with the water. Spread the flour out on another large plate. Remove the chicken from the marinade, shaking off the excess. Coat in the flour, then dip in the egg and coat in the cereal crumbs. If not cooking immediately, arrange on a baking sheet covered with baking parchment.

3 Heat the oil in a large frying pan over a moderate heat. Fry the chicken fingers for 3–4 minutes on each side until they are golden and cooked through. Drain on kitchen paper. Check the temperature before serving.

4 To freeze (uncooked), cover the baking sheet with cling film and freeze for 2–3 hours until firm. Transfer to a sealable plastic bag or box and store in the freezer. Cook from frozen, adding about 30 seconds per side extra cooking time.

overweight children

As your child's eating habits become firmly established, you may become **concerned about her weight**. Overweight toddlers may be on the increase, but as long as **your little one is active** and eating a **healthy, nutritious diet**, you can be sure that she'll put on the correct amount of weight for her individual body type and needs.

Q How can I tell if my young child has a weight problem?

A Again, as discussed in previous chapters, the best way to make an assessment is to use the child growth charts that are supplied by your doctor or health visitor when your baby was born. Keeping tabs on weight by ensuring that your child sits on roughly the same "centile line" as he grows is a very good way to establish whether your child's weight is right for him. If he suddenly jumps up a great deal on the weight front, but his height doesn't show the same change, there may be reason to suspect that he is overweight. BMI charts may also be used by your doctor. A BMI is a number calculated from an individual's weight and height, which is used to determine whether the person is within, or outside of, a normal weight range.

Try not to panic. If your child looks healthy and doesn't have any obvious rolls of fat, his clothing size is appropriate for his age, and no-one has ever made any suggestion that he's overweight, he's probably just fine.

Interestingly, studies have found that most parents are unable to assess accurately when their children do have problems with their weight – ask your doctor or health visitor if you have concerns.

Q Should I put my overweight child on a diet?

A No child, no matter how "overweight" they are, should be put on a diet. The childhood years are extremely important for growth and development, and cutting down on food, or cutting out food groups, can leave a desperate shortfall of important nutrients. Instead, swap over to a healthier diet, with plenty of fresh fruit and vegetables, healthy snacks, and limit foods that are high in unhealthy fats. Add to this a great deal more exercise, and your child will eventually grow into her weight as she becomes taller.

★ is chubby normal?

From babyhood through to five or six years of age, children accumulate more fat on their arms and legs than on their torsos. So dimpled thighs may not be a sign that your child is overweight.

Q Are there any healthy foods that can fill up my child without leading to him becoming overweight?

A The idea is to aim for food that will keep him going throughout the day, and fill his tummy, without adding unnecessary fats or sugars.

The best foods to choose are fresh fruit and vegetables, which have very few calories, but which provide lots of nutrition and energy. Similarly, unrefined carbohydrates, such as wholemeal bread, pasta, and breakfast cereals, and pulses provide an excellent source of energy, and expand to fill the tummy when they are digested.

So aim for pasta dishes with plenty of vegetables, breakfast cereal with lots of fresh fruit, fruit smoothies, toast with nut butters (a source of healthy fats) and a glass of fruit juice, breadsticks and vegetable crudités with fresh dips, and lots of fresh fruit offered throughout the day.

★ active kids

Treat exercise as a priority and ensure that your child is active every day. It's important to make exercise fun and try to include the whole family, when possible – organize a bike ride, a trip to the swimming pool, or just turn on some music and dance – everyone will benefit.

Q My child seems to have a limitless appetite and is putting on weight; how can I encourage her to eat smaller portions?

A First of all, don't immediately assume that weight gain is a sign of impending weight problems. Many kids put on weight just before a growth spurt, and are starving during the same period. They then shoot up, and the weight is redistributed.

However, if you've noticed that your child seems to be eating constantly with no evidence of growth within a month or two, you may need to cut back a little. Offer smaller portions at mealtimes, with the option of more if she's still hungry. She may be in a hurry to get down and get on with her day, and simply eat what's put in front of her. She will also need to learn to recognize her own hunger "cues", and part of that involves recognizing when she's full, and requesting more to eat when she is still hungry. Try offering a drink when she claims to be hungry, as she may simply be thirsty.

You can also make sure that her meals have plenty of fresh fruit and vegetables, which will fill her up without giving her unnecessary calories. Similarly, try to make sure that her snacks are healthy and not filling her up with unhealthy fats or sugar. One or two small, healthy snacks between meals is usually sufficient for the average toddler.

It's also extremely important to ensure that she is active. Very active small children may be very hungry constantly, as regular refuelling is required to sustain high energy levels, but they won't, as a rule, appear to put on weight. If your little one is inactive and still very hungry, the balance may be tipped towards weight problems. Most children have naturally high energy, so try to take advantage of it, and get her going!

food for wellbeing

You may be surprised to notice the impact that your child's diet has on his health and wellbeing; his immunity, moods, sleep patterns, and **ability to concentate can all be affected** by a less-then-ideal diet. With a few tweaks, and an emphasis on fresh, wholesome fare, you'll **soon get him back on track**.

Q Are there signs that my child is not getting adequate nutrition from her diet?

A If your child isn't growing or putting on weight in keeping with her regular centile line on child growth charts (see page 199), her diet may be to blame. A healthy, balanced diet promotes regular growth, and although illness can cause some blips, she should be on roughly the same line throughout her childhood. Deficiencies in vitamins and minerals can cause a number of symptoms, including poor immunity, fatigue, skin problems, muscle cramps, and concentration or behaviour problems.

In particular, children who have difficulty keeping up, and seem listless and low on energy, may not be getting enough iron. If she doesn't eat meat, which is the very best source, offer leafy greens, dried fruit, such as sultanas, dates, and apricots, fish, eggs, fortified breakfast cereals, tofu, pulses, and edible seeds, such as pumpkin or sesame seeds.

She may need a good vitamin and mineral supplement. These provide a little insurance for faddy eaters whose diets are less than ideal. They do not, however, take the place of good nutrition, so continue to offer varied, healthy meals, and consult your doctor if her health doesn't improve.

Q My child always seems tired; could his diet be to blame?

A Yes, it may well be. Firstly, look at how much iron your child is getting (see left).

His diet may also be low in carbohydrates, which provide energy, and too high in refined carbohydrates (for example, white bread, pasta and rice, and cakes and treats), which can play havoc with his blood sugar (you'll notice that he seems almost overly energetic after meals, and then slumps).

Make sure he has plenty of good-quality unrefined carbohydrates such as wholegrain bread, pasta, pulses, and fresh fruit and vegetables. Ideally, he needs at least five or six portions of carbohydrates every day. Try to offer a little protein, such as cheese, lean meat, yogurt, or milk alongside, which slows down the transit of the natural sugars carbohydrates contain, to give a sustained source of energy.

See a doctor if your child's symptoms don't improve.

Q My child is constantly picking up illnesses from nursery school; what food can I give her to help ward off bugs?

A We covered this on page 162, but it's worth repeating as the more sociable your child becomes, the more illnesses she's likely to come into contact with.

Your child needs plenty of vitamin C and other antioxidants every day. Fresh fruit and fruit juices are a great natural source of vitamin C. Tempt her with the smoothie on page 205 too. Brightly coloured fruit and vegetables are a good source of antioxidants, which have an important role to play in optimum nutrition and immunity (see page 163 for more information on these). Consider offering mangos instead of apples, and squash or sweet potato in place of her usual potato. Finally, don't forget oily fish, nuts (chopped), and seeds, which contain EFAs (essential fatty acids) to improve immunity on all levels.

Q Are there any foods to avoid when children have tummy bugs?

A First of all, offer small amounts of food and sips of drinks, which can prevent her tummy being overloaded and making the vomiting or diarrhoea worse. Avoid citrus fruits, which are acidic, but offer plenty of apples and apple juice, instead. These contain pectin, which helps to prevent diarrhoea, and acts as a "prebiotic" to encourage the health of your child's gut. It's a good idea to avoid milk and dairy produce, which can exacerbate the problems, and encourage the build-up of mucus. Bland foods, such as toast, white rice, and rice breakfast cereals are a good choice. It's best to avoid spices, as they can irritate the lining of your child's digestive system.

It's very important to offer plenty of fluid to prevent dehydration. Little sips are better than long drinks, and some children respond better to drinks offered at room temperature, because they are more easily digested. Having said that, if you can't encourage your child to drink much, ice chips and fresh fruit ice lollies (see page 116 for Peach melba lollies) can offer much-needed fluids. An oral rehydration solution may be necessary too, which is available at pharmacies.

★ did you know ...

that you should brush your child's teeth twice a day, at least an hour after she's last eaten, which allows time for her teeth to be remineralized by saliva? (See page 159 for more information.) It's good to encourage her to brush her own teeth, so she gets used to the routine, but you must help, to ensure that they are properly brushed. Keep sweet food and drinks to a minimum, and try to offer them only at mealtimes, when there is plenty of protective saliva swirling around her mouth.

Q Could my toddler's diet be affecting her concentration?

A In much the same way that food could be affecting your toddler's energy levels (see page 201), it could also affect her concentration. If she's eating too many refined carbohydrates, her blood sugar will soar and then plummet, which means she'll be too "hyper" to concentrate when it's high, and too tired when it's low. Unrefined carbohydrates, offered regularly, will ensure steady concentration.

There is also some evidence to suggest that essential fatty acids, in particular, omega 3 oils found in oily fish and flaxseed, can affect concentration levels, in particular with children with autism and ADHD. However, the jury is still out and the research is far from conclusive. It is known, however, that omega-3s are essential for little ones' normal brain development.

Finally, consider whether an iron deficiency could be the cause of your child's poor concentration (see page 201).

Q Are fish oil supplements appropriate for toddlers?

A There are many fish oil supplements designed for toddlers; however these can sometimes be pricey! It is always best to consume omega-3s naturally in oily fish such as salmon, fresh tuna, and mackerel. If your little one has two child-sized portions of oily fish per week, this would provide all the omega-3s that she needs. Other good sources include flaxseeds, olive oil, and squash. However, if your child refuses to eat fish, and isn't tempted by these other sources, you may want to consider a supplement, as omega-3s play an important role in children's brain function and development.

★ food for comfort

Feeding a distressed or upset infant is a natural reaction, as it instantly soothes and calms. It can, however, develop into a habit for both parent and child. Little ones associate food with "feeling better", and we offer it because it works. The problem is that, even as early as toddlerhood, children connect comfort with food, which can lead to "comfort eating". Get into the habit of distracting your child with games or activities, and offer plenty of physical affection to soothe him.

Q Is it possible to develop a food allergy at the age of 24 months?

A Although most food allergies present themselves in infancy, and when the offending foods are first offered, your child may well show the first real signs of food allergy well into her second or third year.

She may have had some niggling reactions that were not noticed or connected with the offending food, for example, or it may be that she hasn't had much contact prior to experiencing a reaction. She may also have a reaction to a food even if she's eaten it before without any problems.

The best advice is to keep on the lookout for any symptoms (see pages 58–59), and see your doctor if she experiences a reaction to a food.

PREPARATION TIME 5 MINUTES | MAKES 2 CHILD PORTIONS, DEPENDING ON AGE AND APPETITE

super c smoothie

Vitamins A and C are good for boosting the immune system, and so is zinc. This smoothie contains **a combination of fruits** that provide these vitamins. **I like to use watermelon**, but you could substitute canteloupe if it is in season and very ripe. **For a thicker smoothie** freeze the strawberries overnight.

115g (4oz) strawberries (3 large or
5 medium), hulled and quartered

1 wedge of watermelon or canteloupe,
seeds and rind removed and
flesh cubed

½ small banana

3 tbsp strawberry yogurt

2 tbsp orange juice

1 tsp clear honey

1 Put everything in a blender and blend until smooth. Pour into a glass and serve straightaway. If there is some smoothie left over, it can be kept in the fridge to drink later – stir it again briefly.

at the table

Over the coming months, your child will begin to develop the **skills, confidence, and understanding** necessary to establish independent eating habits and, of course, **table manners**. It can be a slow process, but with reassurance and guidance, your child will soon be a **polite and self-sufficient** regular at the family table.

Q My toddler just chats and plays games at the table, rather than eating. What should I do?

A Rather that offering an unlimited mealtime, limit it to 20 minutes, after which first courses are taken away, and, desserts (if appropriate) are offered. Also, try to eat as a family, so she can witness how other people behave at the table. Ultimately, if she chooses to play rather than eat, she'll be hungry – it won't take her too long to learn that this gets her nowhere.

⭐ table manners

The truth is that these are not established until children are around five years old. You can, however, gently make suggestions, so that he understands the basics. For example, he has to stay at the table until he's given permission to get down, and he shouldn't talk with his mouth full. If you model the same behaviour yourself, you are much more likely to get somewhere.

Q What's the best way to teach children how to use a knife and fork?

A First of all, choose cutlery designed for little hands and fingers, which are much more manageable. Sit down with your child at mealtimes so she sees how you operate your cutlery. Little ones learn a great deal by copying, and through example, so it's important that you exhibit the table manners you want to see. If her siblings pick up their food, and scoop things up with a spoon rather than using a knife and fork, your child is unlikely to do things any differently.

If she's not too independent, try to feed her some of the time, and then allow her to feed herself. She'll watch the way you spear food with a fork, or use a (blunt) knife to push food onto her fork. She'll see how to negotiate a spoon, and how to turn it to get it into her mouth. Don't worry too much though; it can take little ones months or even years to develop these skills successfully, and to become independent eaters.

Offering some finger food as part of meals can help to encourage hand-eye co-ordination, and reinforce the concept of getting food from plate to mouth. It also helps to ensure that she gets something in her tummy by the end of the meal.

Q **My toddler has tantrums every night at the dinner table; how should I cope with them?**

A Very simply, by ignoring them. As with all tantrums, a child who gets no response will soon see that he needs to adopt a better method. The main reason that toddlers choose to misbehave at mealtimes is because they know that they are bound to get a reaction. You care what they eat, and you mind if they don't eat. What better way to wield an emotional weapon than to hit you where it really hurts! If mealtimes are devoid of emotional charge – in fact, pleasurable and fun – your toddler will not only enjoy them, but soon see that the tantrums have no impact, and, in fact, ruin the fun!

If the tantrums do start, lift him down, don't offer an alternative meal, and try not to lose your temper. You can also help to diffuse the situation by offering some choices in advance, so he feels that he's in control to some extent (see page 180).

Q **How can I encourage my child to stop getting up and down from the table?**

A First of all, when you move your child on to a family chair, make it clear that she is expected to sit until her meal is finished. This isn't a draconian suggestion that she sits there for hours until her plate is empty, but that she does not leave until she is finished. You can catch her and return her to her seat when she escapes, or you can simply remove her meal, so that she learns that leaving the table means that the mealtime is finished, and that there is no more on offer. It might take a couple of hungry evenings for the message to sink in, but it will eventually. Try to encourage her to ask before getting down, which will make life much easier in future.

Q **My toddler still makes a mess when he eats; how can I encourage him to be neater, or does it really matter?**

A Actually, it doesn't really matter. Mess might be annoying but it is a short-term problem and it will soon be a thing of the past.

Try to keep servings small, and give him appropriately sized spoons and forks. Toddlers learn a great deal through experimentation, and they may want to squish food through their fingers, play with it, and use their hands for eating as they explore different tastes, textures, and methods of eating. Be patient and don't assume he's being deliberately messy as he learns to negotiate his food into his mouth; it takes time for fine motor skills to develop. It might help to put a mat under his chair and put a bib on him.

When he spills food or upsets his bowl, gently set it right, and show him how to do it himself. A bowl with a suction cup at the bottom can help too.

It is a different matter if he throws his bowl or food. In this case, remove him from the scene, and he'll soon understand that it is unacceptable. Also, make sure his tummy is empty when he sits down to eat.

time together

Your child will be increasingly curious about food, and will **love to get involved** in family dinners and in the preparation of meals. Even little ones can **help in the kitchen**, and you'll be encouraging good habits and teaching **skills that will last a lifetime**.

Q Can my toddler eat her evening meal with us later in the evening?

A If she's able to wait, and isn't too tired and grumpy, it's a good idea to allow her to eat with you. She'll learn table manners and healthy eating habits, enjoy the sociable aspects of mealtimes, and probably extend her food repertoire in the process.

While eating together is to be encouraged as much as possible, late working hours can make it almost impossible. In this case, don't worry. Sit down with your toddler while she eats, and save family mealtimes for weekends and holidays, until she's old enough for a later bedtime. You can always get her bathed and ready for bed, and offer something light such as fruit and yogurt, or a little toast, when you are ready to eat. Or why not sit her at the table and let her pick at food on your plate? She'll enjoy being a part of what mum and dad do and may be encouraged to try new things.

Q I normally eat later in the evening with my partner, but I'm concerned that meals are becoming a lonely experience for my child. What do you recommend?

A Why not try eating a "starter" with your child, and having a little less later on? If you can manage to eat some of what he is eating, it will be more effective, as he won't feel that he's been sidelined and forced to eat something that no one else has to eat. Or why not make a little salad for you both? He'll be proud to be offered something "adult" (even if he only eats a little). Make sure you at least sit with him to ensure mealtimes are a sociable experience.

Q What foods can I introduce to appeal to the whole family?

A As long as family meals are healthy and balanced, anything goes. Experiment with new flavours from other cuisines, such as Indian, Italian, or Turkish, and add fun and variety to your diet. Try, also, to forget the idea that there are "kid" foods and "adult" foods – anything can be adapted to different levels of sophistication. My chicken meatballs (page 216) can, for example, be made into a Thai meatball meal with noodles for the rest of the family.

Q Will sitting at the family table encourage my child to try new things?

A It will undoubtedly make a difference. First of all, it provides quality time with your child, and encourages her to think of food and mealtimes as a positive experience. This goes a long way towards preventing faddy eating habits.

Secondly, studies show that kids who eat with their parents regularly have a much better idea of what foods are healthy, and are more likely to be adventurous eaters. They learn table manners, and social etiquette, and pick up your values. In terms of new foods, kids are much more likely to try foods that everyone else is eating, as they want to be equal and "important".

Furthermore, parents and siblings act as role models, and all children are keen to copy. Displaying your own healthy eating habits can be invaluable for your child, and encourage her to follow suit. If everyone is eating the same food, she'll be much more likely to try them herself. Be patient, though. If you have extended family meals your child might become bored and irritable. Most young children will have eaten their fill in about 20 minutes, so allow her to be "released", to play on the kitchen floor, or sit on a parent's lap.

Q How can I get my child involved in the kitchen?

A From the very early days it's a good idea to encourage your little one to help out in the kitchen, from sieving, mixing, grating, and cracking eggs, to rolling out dough and cutting out shapes (see Mini jam tarts; page 193). Children also enjoy being involved in setting the table and helping to put together a salad, stirring the salad dressing, or spreading butter on bread.

Q Do you have some fun recipes that my child and I can create together?

A Making cakes is always popular – involve him in making the Cupcake caterpillar cake (page 218), or the White chocolate crispie squares (page 212). He'll enjoy adding his own toppings to mini pizzas (see Cheese and ham pit-zas; page 142), dipping fish goujons in breadcrumbs (page 138), or making his own fruit ice lollies (page 116).

★ did you know ...

that your child is much more likely to eat something that she's played a part in making? Children view their accomplishments with huge pride, and will take great interest in the reaction they get from you. If you all sit down and eat happily, she'll undoubtedly do the same, even if she's fully aware that some of the ingredients are on her usual "I won't eat" list. What's more, she'll learn to understand the steps involved in preparing food, a little about nutrition, and will develop her tastes.

⭐ **condiments?**

It's fine to introduce condiments to your little one. Mustard, ketchup (see below), fresh pickles, salsa, mayonnaise, pesto, and even non-MSG chilli dips are all appropriate for little ones. Remember, though, that toddlers have very small tummies, and adding extra sauces or ingredients is likely to fill them up even more quickly, preventing ideal nutritional intake from their healthy diets, so offer them only in small quantities.

Q Is it OK to give my child a little ketchup?

A Despite its rather tawdry reputation, there is absolutely nothing wrong with ketchup. In the past, ketchup tended to be high in salt and sugar, but many newer brands are much lower in these additives, and much tastier as a result.

Ketchup is, actually, healthy, too. A number of studies have found that it is a useful addition to any diet, because it contains a substance called lycopene. Lycopene is especially concentrated in tomato sauce and paste, and is an antioxidant (these cancel out the effects of free radicals, which damage the body's genetic material and can lead to cancer and a host of other illnesses). What's more, lycopene helps to improve eyesight, and encourages a healthy heart. So a little salt and sugar do not detract from its clear benefits.

Q How can I sweeten foods without using too much sugar?

A First of all, white sugar is the worst of the lot, so even using brown or unrefined sugars can make a difference. Maple syrup and honey all have plenty of nutrients, which make them a healthy option. They sweeten but also add some vitamins and minerals (and, in the case of honey, some antibacterial properties), whereas sugar is often simply empty calories. Molasses, barley malt syrup, brown rice syrup, fruit juice, fruit purées, and agave syrup – a very sweet, natural source of sugar, derived from a plant – are all healthy options. Whatever you do, don't resort to artificial sweeteners, which may not add any calories, or damage teeth, but offer absolutely no nutrients and may have a negative impact on health.

Q My child seems to have developed a taste for salt, and won't eat anything without a generous sprinkling. What should I do?

A There is no doubt that salt can make things taste nicer, and that it is addictive! If you started him off on jarred foods with added salt, or he's become accustomed to salty snacks, fresh healthy food will undoubtedly taste bland and unappealing. There are a few ways round this. Firstly, try to make his food more flavourful by adding herbs, spices, juice, wine, and low-sodium stocks when cooking. If he gets lots of flavour, he won't miss the salty taste. For ideas on flavouring kids' food, see page 145. Try also, as a family, to leave the salt shaker off the table. If no one else is doing it, and there is no shaker in evidence, he'll likely forget, and the habit will be broken.

PREPARATION TIME 25 MINUTES | COOKING TIME 20–25 MINUTES | MAKES 8 (OR 16 COCKTAIL SIZE)

chicken sausage rolls

Elevate your family picnic to new heights by serving these delicious chicken rolls instead of the usual sandwiches. Take along a small pot of ketchup for **dipping the sausage rolls**.

1 tbsp olive oil

½ small red onion, finely chopped

1 small carrot, peeled and grated

½ small garlic clove, crushed

¼ tsp fresh thyme leaves

1 slice of bread, crust removed

115g (4oz) minced chicken

1 tbsp tomato ketchup

2 tbsp grated Parmesan cheese

Salt and freshly ground black pepper

225g (8oz) shortcrust pastry

1 egg, beaten

1 Heat the oil in a small frying pan, add the onion and carrot, and cook for about 3 minutes or until softened. Add the garlic and cook for 1 minute, then stir in the thyme and set aside. Put the bread in a food processor and process to crumbs. Add the onion mixture, chicken, tomato ketchup, and Parmesan and season with salt and pepper. Pulse to combine (you can also mix by hand in a bowl).

2 Preheat the oven to 200°C (180°C fan), gas 6. Cut the pastry in half and roll out each half on a lightly floured surface to a 12 x 18cm (5 x 7in) rectangle. Halve the chicken mixture and roll each into a sausage 18cm (7in) long. Put one in the centre of each piece of pastry and brush the edges of the pastry with beaten egg. Wrap the pastry over the sausage to overlap down the back. Press gently to seal, then turn over. Cut each roll into four and place seam-side down on a baking sheet. Brush with egg and cut two small slits in the top of each.

3 Bake for 20–25 minutes until golden brown. Transfer to a wire rack to cool. Keep in the fridge for up to 2 days, or freeze and thaw at room temperature. The rolls can be reheated in a very low oven for 8–10 minutes.

PREPARATION TIME ABOUT 10 MINUTES | MAKES 9 LARGE OR 16 SMALL SQUARES

white chocolate crispie squares

These are **so simple and easy**, but I haven't found anyone yet who doesn't love this variation on an old favourite. They are great for parties too. They **don't take long to prepare** and you can have a lot of fun making them with your child.

100g (3½oz) white chocolate

100g (3½oz) unsalted butter

3 tbsp golden syrup

Pinch of salt

100g (3½oz) puffed rice cereal

30g (1oz) rolled oats

50g (1¾oz) exotic dried fruits, chopped or dried apricots, chopped

1 Break the chocolate into pieces and put in a large saucepan with the butter, golden syrup, and salt. Melt over a low heat. Remove from the heat and stir in the puffed rice cereal and oats. Fold in the dried fuits. If adding mini marshmallows (see variations below), allow the mixture to cool down before folding these in.

2 Line a 20cm (8in) square shallow baking tin with non-stick baking parchment, cutting the paper large enough to extend above the sides of the tin.

3 Spoon the mixture into the tin and press down lightly with a potato masher or spatula to level the surface. Cover and chill in the fridge to set. Cut into squares before serving. Store in the fridge.

★ **Variations:** Replace the exotic dried fruit or dried apricots with raisins, or omit the fruit and use 30g (1oz) mini marshmallows. For adults I like to add 30g (1oz) chopped pecan nuts.

your sociable child

As your toddler grows older and her **social net widens**, she'll begin to **make her own friends**, and undoubtedly be influenced by them! Parties, too, may be a more prominent feature of your child's life. **With a little creativity**, you can **continue to offer nutritious**, delicious food, and broaden your child's palate in the process.

Q **My child is starting to have friends round for lunch and tea; do you have any good ideas for toddler-friendly meals?**

A Most little ones won't want to spend a lot of time at the table, and will be keen to bolt down their food and get on with the fun. It makes sense, therefore, to offer small, manageable portions of food that look fun to eat.

Pasta is always popular with little ones – spoon a hidden vegetable sauce on top (page 183) or add chicken meatballs (page 216). For kids at the older end of this age group, you can make a little pasta "bar" with some grated cheese, cooked peas, sweetcorn, little meatballs, diced chicken, tuna, olives, and tomato sauce so that they can create their own pasta masterpieces.

Other good ideas are platters of toddler-sized sandwiches with fruit and some mini muffins (see page 197) or flapjacks (see page 157), mini meat or fish balls (see page 216 for Chicken meatballs), mini burgers (see page 185), marinated chicken skewers (see page 150), individual fish or shepherd's pies, or even a baked potato with one of any number of toppings. Little quiches or mini pizzas (see page 142) make a nice treat too.

It can sometimes be difficult to encourage fussier eaters to get on with the vegetables, but supplying crudités with a tasty dip alongside is a solution.

★ did you know ...

that you can make healthy versions of more traditional kids' foods? Serve fish goujons (see page 138) or chicken fingers (see page 198) rather than "nuggets", mini burgers (see page 185), and pasta with tomato sauce (see page 183). Although your little one may express interest in the less-healthy foods that his friends eat, the trick is to never give in. If you always offer healthy, nutritious food, he'll develop a taste for them, and see them as familiar.

Q Should I ring parents to check that visitors don't have food allergies?

A In reality, it's up to the parents of allergic children to contact you if there are problems with food, and even send their own if there is potential for a reaction. However, if you are having a child around for the first time, it's best to check. Some parents might just assume that everyone knows their child is allergic, and forget to mention it.

Q How can my child explain to her friends that she doesn't eat meat?

A I would suggest that she doesn't need to do this herself, and that you can advise parents or carers of this fact in advance. There are plenty of child-friendly meals that do not include meat, including pastas, salads, sandwiches, and soups. If the adults are aware of your child's diet, they can make the appropriate choices without any need for explanation.

If your child does find that she's in the position of having to refuse something because it is meat or it contains meat, you can encourage her to explain that she either doesn't "like" meat, or that her family doesn't "eat" it. Most young children aren't self-conscious enough to mind saying that they like, or don't eat, different things.

Your child may slip up and eat meat on the odd occasion, and even start to demand it – whether or not you allow this is your choice. But if you are staunch about your vegetarian beliefs, then simply explain to your child that you have different eating habits in your family.

When you invite her friends to tea, avoid offering anything that might put off the average toddler. Stick to a vegetarian meal that most children would eat at home, such as pasta with tomato sauce.

Q It's my child's third birthday coming up – do you have any ideas for healthy party foods?

A Traditional birthday party food doesn't have to be unhealthy, and you can create delicious cakes, muffins, and biscuits using honey, molasses, and brown sugar to sweeten them, or add grated carrots, courgettes, apples, or pears to make them moist and nutritious.

Pretty, tiny, and brightly coloured are the order of the day, and you'll be a step closer to getting them to eat what you want. Platters of fresh fruit with chocolate sauce for dipping are fun, as are bite-sized pieces of fruit threaded onto a straw. Little pizzas with faces on English muffins or mini pittas (see page 142) can "hide" quite a few veggies in the toppings.

Fresh fruit ice lollies (see page 116) are perfect for outside parties. Smoothies (see page 205) offered in tiny shot glasses are ideal for offering a boost of nutrition, and some much needed fluid.

One-bite sandwich squares are most appealing to little ones, as are mini bagels. For filling ideas, see page 191. Create tiny salads inside a baby gem lettuce leaf, with just enough for one or two bites. Breadsticks with hummus, cheese straws, and chunks of cheese are always popular.

PREPARATION TIME 25 MINUTES | COOKING TIME 30 MINUTES | MAKES 5–6 CHILD PORTIONS

chicken meatballs with tomato sauce

Pasta and tomato sauce **usually goes down well** with small children. I have added some delicious mini chicken meatballs that can be **mashed into the sauce** if anyone isn't keen on "lumps"!

1 tbsp olive oil

1 red onion, finely chopped

1 small carrot, peeled and grated

1 eating apple, cored and grated

1 garlic clove, crushed

2 tsp balsamic vinegar

2 tsp soft light brown sugar

1 tsp thyme leaves or chopped parsley

400g (14oz) can chopped tomatoes

2 tbsp tomato purée

1 tbsp tomato ketchup

120ml (4fl oz) vegetable stock

20g (¾oz) fresh breadcrumbs

1 tbsp apple juice or apple sauce

225g (8oz) minced chicken

3 tbsp grated Parmesan cheese

1–2 tbsp plain flour, for dusting

2–3 tbsp sunflower oil, for frying

Per portion:

30–45g (1–1½oz) fusilli, cooked

1 Heat the olive oil in a large saucepan and cook the onion, carrot, and apple until soft and golden. Add the garlic and cook for 1 minute, then add the vinegar and 1 tsp of the sugar. Cook, stirring, until the vinegar has evaporated. Add the thyme. Spoon half of the onion mixture into a large bowl and set aside.

2 Add the tomatoes, tomato purée, ketchup, stock, and the remaining sugar to the onion mixture in the pan. Season to taste with salt and pepper. Bring to the boil, then reduce the heat and simmer gently for 20 minutes, stirring occasionally.

3 Meanwhile, make the meatballs by adding the breadcrumbs, apple juice, chicken, and Parmesan to the onion mixture in the bowl. Mix well and season. For a finer texture, chop everything together in a food processor. Dust your hands with flour and roll teaspoonfuls of the chicken mixture into 28 small meatballs that are the size of large cherry tomatoes.

4 Heat the sunflower oil in a large non-stick frying pan and brown the meatballs for about 1 minute on each side. Remove from the pan with a fish slice and drain on kitchen paper.

5 Add the meatballs to the sauce, cover, and simmer for a further 10 minutes or until cooked through. Divide the meatballs into portions and toss very gently with a portion of cooked pasta. Cool slightly before serving with extra Parmesan.

6 The meatballs and sauce (without pasta) can be kept in the fridge, covered, for up to 2 days, or frozen in individual portions; thaw overnight in the fridge. Reheat in a small pan or microwave, adding 1 tsp water per portion if necessary. Toss with freshly cooked pasta and serve as above.

PREPARATION TIME 1½ HOURS | COOKING TIME 20 MINUTES | CUTS INTO 15–23 PORTIONS

cupcake caterpillar

Here's **a fun and easy idea** for a second or third birthday party. You can expand your caterpillar according to the number of guests at your party, and **decorate it however you like**.

Cupcakes

175g (6oz) softened unsalted butter

175g (6oz) caster sugar

3 eggs

1½ tsp vanilla extract

175g (6oz) self-raising flour

Pinch of salt

Buttercream icing

115g (4oz) softened butter

225g (8oz) icing sugar, sifted

¼ tsp vanilla extract

Red, dark green, light green, and
  yellow food colouring

Decoration

Thin black liquorice lace

1 black liquorice allsort

1 mini marshmallow

2 silver balls

6–8 chocolate mini rolls

Smarties and jelly beans

1 Preheat the oven to 180°C (160°C fan), gas 4. Line 15 small muffin or tartlet tins with paper cases.

2 To make the cupcakes, cream together the butter and sugar until pale and fluffy. Add the rest of the ingredients and beat until just combined. Divide among the paper cases. Bake for about 20 minutes or until risen and golden and the centres spring back when lightly pressed. Cool in the tins briefly, then transfer to a wire rack to cool completely.

3 To make the buttercream, beat the butter until pale, then beat in the icing sugar a little at a time, followed by the vanilla extract. Scoop a rounded tablespoon of the icing into a small bowl and colour it red. Colour half of the remaining icing dark green and the rest light green.

4 To make the head, ice one of the cupcakes with the red buttercream. Cut two antennae from the liquorice lace and a nose from the liquorice allsort. For the eyes, cut a mini marshmallow in half and colour the cut side with a cocktail stick dipped in yellow food colouring. Add a silver ball to the centre and press to stick on. Position the antennae, nose, and eyes on the head and add a mouth in liquorice lace. Leave to set.

5 Ice half of the remaining cupcakes with dark green buttercream and half with light green buttercream. Put a line of mini rolls along the bottom of a large board (such as a chopping board covered in foil) to make a tree branch. Position the cupcakes to resemble a caterpillar waffling along the branch. Make markings on the caterpillar's back with Smarties, jelly beans, or thin strips of liquorice, sticking them into the buttercream at angles. If you like, add red jelly beans for the caterpillar's feet.

resources

consultants

General

akTV
www.annabelkarmel.tv
The Annabel Karmel online internet TV channel has step-by-step videos of recipes, advice, and top tips, including interviews with top experts on subjects like food allergies, and with parents on common feeding issues.

Annabel Karmel
www.annabelkarmel.com
The no. 1 site for child nutrition. It includes recipes for all occasions, as well as advice and top tips on nutrition. There is also a very popular online community for parents and carers.

Babycentre
www.babycentre.co.uk
An online community for new parents, offering information on all aspects of childcare up to 36 months.

National Childcare Trust
www.nct.org.uk
This website provides articles on a range of topics, as well as helplines, including breastfeeding counselling.

Allergy

Allergy UK
www.allergyuk.org
A national medical charity dealing with allergy, which provides information on allergy, intolerance, and chemical sensitivity.

Anaphylaxis Campaign
www.anaphylaxis.org.uk
A charity that helps people with life-threatening allergic reactions to foods.

Breastfeeding

Association of Breastfeeding Mothers
www.abm.me.uk
Ran by mothers for mothers, giving helpful advice and accurate information to mothers who breastfeed.

Breastfeeding Network
www.breastfeedingnetwork.org.uk
A source of support and information for breastfeeding mums.

La Leche League
www.lalecheleague.org.uk
An organization to encourage mother-to-mother support for breastfeeding.

Equipment

Lakeland Limited
www.lakeland.co.uk

Mothercare
www.mothercare.com

Nutrition and health

British Dietetic Association
www.bda.uk.com
Provides practical guidance to enable people to make appropriate lifestyle and food choices.

British Nutrition Foundation
www.nutrition.org.uk
Provides healthy eating information and recipes.

Food Standards Agency
www.food.gov.uk
A useful website for understanding labelling rules and regulations.

NHS Direct
www.nhsdirect.nhs.uk
Contains information about conditions, treatments, and services for all types of conditions. Includes a self-help guide and 24-hour helpline: 0845 4647.

Vegan Society
www.vegansociety.com
Useful information on nutrition and bringing up vegan children.

Vegetarian Society
www.vegsoc.org
Offers recipes and advice on nutrition, approved products, and eating out.

Dr Adam Fox MA(Hons), MSc, MB, BS, DCH, FRCPCH, Dip Allergy, FHEA
Adam is one of the UK's leading Paediatric Allergists and works as a consultant at Guy's & St Thomas' Hospital in London. He has a particular interest in food allergy and eczema. Adam was named Paediatric Allergist of the year by the charity Allergy UK in 2007.
www.adamfox.co.uk

Dr Su Laurent MRCP FRCPCH
Su is Consultant Paediatrician at Barnet Hospital, London, where she supervizes the medical care of children of all ages, from extremely premature babies to teenagers. A medical advisor to and regular presenter on the Baby Channel, she is also expert paediatrician for *Mother & Baby* magazine. She has also written books on parenting and child health for Dorling Kindersley.

Dr Rosan Meyer MSc Diet, M. Nutrition, PhD
Rosan is a specialist paediatric dietitian from Imperial College, London. She has her own dietetic practice and specializes in allergies, intolerances, and feeding problems. She regularly writes articles for health journals on infant and toddler nutrition and is an expert on several government nutrition panels.

Joanna Moorhead
Joanna is an author and journalist. She writes on health and parenting for *The Guardian* and *The Times* and is a regular contributor to TV and radio programmes on parenting issues, including the Jeremy Vine show on Radio 2 and BBC Breakfast News on BBC1. She has a special interest in breastfeeding and breastfed each of her own four children to the age of two, including her first child who was born two months prematurely.

index

about the author

Annabel Karmel MBE is the leading authority on nutrition and cooking for children and her bestselling books are sold all over the world. A mother of three, Annabel is well known for providing advice and guidance to millions of parents on what to feed their children, as well as getting families to eat a healthier diet without spending hours in the kitchen.

Annabel writes regularly for newspapers and magazines and appears frequently on radio and TV as the UK's top expert on children's nutrition. She has several ranges of healthy ready meals in supermarkets, including her *Eat Fussy* range for one to four year olds and her *Make It Easy* range of sauces and pastas. She also has an innovative range of equipment to help parents prepare baby food. Her healthy meals are also served in all of the leading theme parks in the UK, including Alton Towers and Legoland, the largest group of nurseries, and a chain of family-based holiday parks.

Her popular website www.annabelkarmel.com is the number one online destination for child nutrition, featuring advice, delicious recipes, and social networking.

acknowledgments

Author's acknowledgments

I'd like to thank Peggy Vance at DK for making it such fun to work on this book; Caroline Stearns for working with me and testing all the yummy recipes; Dave King and Michael Birt for their stunning photography; Seiko Hatfield and Katie Giovanni for their food styling; Elizabeth Jones for keeping my business running while I wrote this book; Evelyn Etkind, my mum, for tasting my recipes – even the baby purees!; Marina Magpoc Abaigar and Letty Catada for helping me in the kitchen; Mary Jones, my loyal publicist; Dr Adam Fox, Consultant Paediatric Allergist; Dr Rosan Meyer, Specialist Dietitian at Imperial College, London; Dr Su Laurent, Consultant Paediatrician at Barnet Hospital, London; Joanna Moorhead for her breastfeeding advice; all the models; and the wonderful team at DK: Helen Murray, Sarah Ponder, Charlotte Seymour, Esther Ripley, Penny Warren, Marianne Markham, Glenda Fisher, and Caroline Gibson.

Publisher's acknowledgments

DK would like to thank Louisa Grey for prop styling; Susan Bosanko for the index; Irene Lyford for proofreading; Andrea Baynham for editorial assistance; Adam Brackenbury for artworking; and our models: Amber Asamoa; Kai Brogan; Lachlan Bush; Dexter Channer; Ava, Humaira and John Felton; Leo Hayward; Tarin Houston; Jas Kang; Hazel and Noah Loo; Elisa and Jolie Margolin; Oliver Moore; Rosina Morris; Nicola Munn; Kyra Nelson; Freddie and Sharon Ortiz; Alex Smith; Aurelia Stearns; Luke and Rhonda Summerbell; Heidi Taylor and Olivia Taylor-Clarkson; Elliot Tripp; Darcy Williams; Daisy and Zoe Wood; Lilyann Yuen-Dent.

Picture credits

The publisher would like to thank the following for their kind permission to reproduce their photographs: **Corbis:** Bloomimage 202; **Getty Images:** Tom Grill 164; Fraser Hall 22; **Photolibrary:** Banana Stock 141, 181; Blend 132; Digital Vision 62; Fancy 17; Gaurier Gaurier 83; Stockbyte 12; **SuperStock:** age fotostock 35 All other images © Dorling Kindersley For further information see: www.dkimages.com